The CDC Handbook – a guide to cleaning and disinfecting cleanrooms

2nd edition

Edited by Dr. Tim Sandle

Grosvenor House Publishing Limited

This book is published by
Grosvenor House Publishing Ltd
28-30 High Street, Guildford, Surrey, GU1 3EL.
www.grosvenorhousepublishing.co.uk

Printed in the United Kingdom.

A CIP record for this book
is available from the British Library

ISBN 978-1-78148-768-6

ACKNOWLEDGEMENTS

This book was developed with an unrestricted educational grant from schülke. All proceeds from the sale of this book will go towards research, training and education in relation to healthcare associated infections.

The editor would like to express his thanks to Jane Stevenson for her invaluable help in bringing this book to fruition.

CONTENTS

ABOUT THE EDITOR

Tim SANDLE, PhD: Tim Sandle has twenty-five years experience as a pharmaceutical microbiologist. Dr. Sandle is an honorary consultant with the School of Pharmacy and Pharmaceutical Sciences, University of Manchester and is a tutor for the university's pharmaceutical microbiology M.Sc course. Dr. Sandle serves on several national and international committees relating to pharmaceutical microbiology and cleanroom contamination control (including the ISO cleanroom standards). He is a long-standing committee member of the Pharmaceutical Microbiology Interest Group (Pharmig). Dr. Sandle authored over three hundred book chapters, peer reviewed papers and technical articles and has delivered papers to over seventy international conferences. This is his tenth book. Dr. Sandle operates a popular pharmaceutical and healthcare discussion blog at http://www.pharmamicroresources.com

ABOUT THE AUTHORS

Laura BUCK: Laura Buck has a first class honours degree in Biochemistry from the University of Bath and was awarded a doctorate in neuroscience at University College London followed by a role in medical communications at Health Interactions.

Amit CHANDRA: Amit Chandra has been at Loughborough in various engineering roles including working to develop new therapies for post-surgery and post-trauma maxillofacial reconstruction in a hospital setting. Currently Amit is focussing on validating a cleanroom facility for Loughborough University as the Engineering Team Leader at the Cell Therapy Manufacturing Facility (CTMF) at the Centre for Biological Engineering at Loughborough University. The facility (currently in validation) provides both the physical requirements and technical expertise to aseptically culture, expand, differentiate and harvest human adherent cells to be used for the preparation of GMP compliant batches of somatic cell therapies and tissue engineered products using an automated cell culture platform.

Eric CHE: Eric Che, MPharmS, FTQA Dip, is the Principal Pharmacist at Quality Assurance, St Georges

Hospital. Eric is a Quality Assurance pharmacist with experience in providing QA support and consultancy service to a range of MHRA licensed and unlicensed aseptic units. Eric's Quality Assurance team provides a room HPV decontamination service to St Georges Healthcare NHS Trust in liaison with infection control and facilities.

James DRINKWATER: James Drinkwater is the Chairman (from 2012) of the Pharmaceutical and Healthcare Sciences Society (PHSS) and a specialist in hydrogen peroxide vapour decontamination at Bioquell UK. His areas of specialist knowledge include aseptic processing, freeze drying, separation barrier technology and environmental monitoring.

Ian M. JARVIS: Ian Jarvis graduated in 1991 with an honours degree in Chemistry followed in 1994 by a post graduate diploma in Industrial Pharmaceutical Studies. He has been an acting Qualified Person for 15 years and worked in areas as diverse as Quality Assurance, Production Management and R&D.

Ian has a strong background in the pharmaceutical industry having worked for two major pharmaceutical companies within the last 25 years. He currently holds a position within R&D and has responsibility for the QA aspects of externalisation, covering manufacturing, distribution, release of investigational medicinal products and auditing of global clinical pharmacology units. He is a Chartered Chemist, a member of the Royal Society of Chemistry and the Parenteral Drug Association.

Angela NUTMAN: Angela Nutman BSc (Pharmacy) (University of Brighton), Post graduate diploma in Clinical Pharmacy Practice (London School of Pharmacy), MSc Pharmaceutical Technology and Quality Assurance (University of Leeds). Angela is the Assistant Director of Pharmacy (Technical Services) at Lancashire Teaching Hospitals NHS Foundation Trust. Angela's previous experience includes QA Team Manager at Leeds Teaching Hospitals NHS Foundation Trust; Lead Pharmacist Aseptic Services Education and Training – Leeds Teaching Hospitals NHS Foundation Trust; Aseptic Services Manager at York Teaching Hospitals NHS Foundation Trust; Specialist Oncology Pharmacist at Guys and St Thomas NHS Foundation Trust; Clinical Pharmacist at King Edward VII Hospital, Midhurst; Rotational Pharmacist at Royal West Sussex NHS Trust and at Chichester and Royal Marsden Teaching Hospitals NHS Trust, London.

Tim SANDLE: Tim Sandle. BSc (Hons), M.A., PhD. Tim Sandle is the Head of Microbiology at Bio Products Laboratory. BPL manufactures aseptic products and has a suite of over 200 cleanrooms. Tim is experienced in receiving MHRA and FDA inspections.

Jasdeep SINGH: Jasdeep Singh. BSc (Hons) Physiology 1994 from UCL; BSc (Hons) Pharmacy 1998 University of Brighton. Qualified as a Pharmacist in 1999. Jasdeep is Head of Pharmaceutical Manufacturing Unit at Barts and the London NHS trust, a role he has undertaken since 2006.

FOREWORD

Founded in 1889 by Rudolf Schülke and Julius Mayr, Schülke & Mayr GmbH originates from the pioneers of modern hygiene and preservation. Since 1996 Schülke & Mayr GmbH has been part of the Air Liquide Group – world leader in gases for industry, health and the environment. It is the aim of our business to protect people and materials against infections and contaminations. To achieve this, we provide innovative technologies, highly effective products and expert support services in the specialist sectors of hygiene and special preservation. In doing so, we can rely on an all-embracing knowledge and a long tradition of innovation. It is therefore, a great honour for us to be involved in the planning and support of such a worthy project. The editor and the authors selected are experts in their respective fields and have had one guiding principle: to produce a reliable, current and convenient handbook to provide the best information about the safe use of detergents and disinfectants in cleanrooms and hospitals. We recognize that this edition would not have been possible without the capable input of the authors and are deeply grateful to all individuals who participated in making this book a reality.

Dr. Peter Goroncy-Bermes
International Scientific Management
AirLiquide International Expert
Schülke & Mayr GmbH, Norderstedt

INTRODUCTION

By Tim Sandle

Contamination control is of great importance to healthcare facilities and to pharmaceutical cleanrooms. With healthcare, the more immediate concern is with protecting the patient from infection (infection prevention practices aim to eliminate the risk of the transmission of pathogens between patients and between patients and the health care worker). With pharmaceuticals the concern is with avoiding contamination of the product being prepared so that the product is safe for use. Both healthcare facilities (from hospital wards to pharmacy units) and pharmaceutical facilities share a number of similarities, from the importance of hand sanitisation to the control of cleanrooms.

The key interconnecting aspect is the use of cleaning agents (detergents) and disinfectants. Therefore designing an effective cleaning and disinfection programme is a critical part of the contamination control approach. Whilst there are a myriad of different agents on the marketplace, not all are suitable for cleanrooms, hands or hospital wards. To add to this there is a sometimes bewildering choice of different chemicals with different modes of action, many of which are incompatible with one another. From this there is often ambiguity about how such agents should be used including questions of 'how often should I use this?', 'how do I dilute it?', 'how long do I leave it for?' coupled with confusion over cleaning methods and techniques. In relation to these issues it became clear that there was no book, of smaller size, which addressed these issues for those concerned with keeping hospitals and cleanrooms clean. In light of this, the idea for this book - "*The Cleaning and Disinfection Handbook*" - was born.

This book has two approaches and two aims. In terms of its aims, the book is designed to provide information of interest to those who work in cleanrooms, for pharmaceutical manufacturing or within a hospital setting, and for those who need to be aware of contamination control issues within health care settings (from the ward to the pharmacy). The book is designed for the specialist and non-specialist alike, and will also be of interest to the general public who have an interest in or concern about how cleanrooms, hospitals and the staff who work within them seek to control contamination through the use of cleaning materials and disinfectants. To help the less experienced reader the book contains a glossary of terms, which can be found at the end of the book.

In terms of the approach, the book aims to balance the theoretical with the practical and the reader will see that most of the chapters marry these two approaches. Most of the chapters begin with an introduction to the science behind what is happening (the microbiology and the chemistry) and then move on to show how such scientific principles can be applied to the 'real life' practical situations in which hospital staff and cleanroom operators deal with each working day. Depending upon the subject matter of the chapter, some chapters lean towards the more theoretical and some towards the more practical. This is shown partially by a short review of each chapter.

In the first chapter of the book Tim Sandle presents an overview of principles and definitions of cleaning, detergents and disinfectants. The aim of the chapter is to provide a straightforward understanding for those less familiar with the different types of detergents and disinfectants available, how they interact, and some of the issues of importance in relation to their use including contact times, spectrum of activity, temperatures of use, material compatibility and the properties of microcidal efficacy. The chapter also discusses resistance of microorganisms to disinfectant agents.

In the second chapter, Ian Jarvis addresses an area of great importance to contamination control: hand sanitisation. Hands which have a low level of contamination are essential to health care, especially as a means of slowing down Hospital Acquired Infections. So too is the need for gloved hands to carry a low level of contamination in relation to hospital surgery units and within cleanrooms used for pharmaceutical processing. In the chapter, hand sanitisers (applied to gloved hands) and antiseptics (applied to skin) are outlined. The chapter also examines the common skin based microorganisms and the different types of disinfectants available (alcohol based and non-alcohol sanitisers). From a practical perspective, the chapter underlines the importance of the techniques of hand rubbing and wiping and demonstrates this with some very useful illustrations.

The third chapter examines the selection of cleaning materials. In this chapter, Jasdeep Singh outlines the factors to consider when selecting the appropriate cleaning materials to use including mops, wipes and buckets. The materials considered relate to both healthcare and pharmaceutical cleanrooms. A strong emphasis is placed on selecting the right materials and in not re-using materials. Underlying this is the premise that if the cleaning materials are of poor quality, then the processes of cleaning and disinfection will also be of poor quality and the reduction of microorganisms will consequently be inefficient.

Following on from cleaning materials, the subject of the fourth chapter is cleaning techniques. In this chapter Angela Nutman covers a number of important aspects of cleaning. These include the preparation of disinfectant solutions and the importance of the correct dilution. In terms of sound cleaning methods the double and triple bucket methods are outlined. Considerable emphasis is placed upon learning in the correct sequence: such as removing dust beforehand; the importance of applying detergent before disinfection; observing contact times; concerns with residues; and the practical way to clean an area without re-introducing contamination. Within the chapter, reference is also made to the importance of staff training.

Whilst many disinfectants are effective biocides they can be of concern to the staff tasked with using them in terms of health and safety. The safe use of detergents and disinfectants is the concern of the fifth chapter. In this chapter Ian Jarvis makes reference to national and international regulations such as the Biocide Products Directive and to the importance of chemical health and safety risk assessments and of understanding occupational health and exposure hazards. The chapter also discusses the importance of protective personal equipment and waste management and disposal procedures.

There are important differences as well as different concerns to the way in which contamination control programmes apply to hospitals in contrast to pharmaceutical facilities. Chapters six and eight present these differences.

In chapter six, Eric Che looks at the application of disinfectants and detergents in the healthcare setting. The chapter outlines how detergents and disinfectants are used in hospitals and some of the important concerns which hospitals face, such as the risk of nosocomial infections and the relationship between Hospital Acquired Infection and infection control. The chapter also considers the types of things that need cleaning and disinfection, focusing upon the types of things likely to become contaminated as well as with the types of microorganisms found that are of concern.

Chapter seven is soundly practically based and presents model procedures for the cleaning and disinfection of a small unit. The chapter is presented as a case study and will allow those who work in smaller facilities to compare approaches. In the chapter Amit Chandra discusses essential elements including the preparation of cleaning agents, staff gowning, cleaning methods and training requirements.

Cleanrooms within the pharmaceutical industry are the concern of chapter eight. In this chapter Tim Sandle places cleaning and disinfection within the pharmaceutical context. In the chapter the importance, from a Good Manufacturing Practice standpoint, of disinfectant rotation is explained as well as the importance of material compatibility trials and factors which primarily only affect aseptic areas, such as the importance of sterile disinfectants. The chapter also considers how it can be proven, practically, that disinfectants are keeping contamination control in check. For this, the chapter argues for the necessity of conducting field trials and for assessing the effectiveness of such trials by conducting microbiological environmental monitoring.

Chapter nine addresses a different aspect of disinfection, moving away from the manual cleaning techniques, and towards gaseous disinfection. In this chapter James Drinkwater and Laura Buck look at the use of hydrogen peroxide vapour and its use within cleanrooms and its increasing application for the surface disinfection of barrier systems (such as isolators). Due to the importance of gaseous disinfection where a sporicidal reduction step is required, the chapter outlines the use of biological indicators as the primary means of verification.

Chapter ten is the final chapter of the book. In this chapter Tim Sandle discusses the importance of disinfectant validation which is important from a regulatory perspective and also on the part of the user in having confidence that the disinfectants are reducing the microbial population (and eliminating the intended types of microorganisms) to the levels required. In outlining the essentials of validation, the chapter compares and contrasts European and U.S. approaches to validation.

In putting this book together some of the leading experts in the field of contamination control, working either within health care or the pharmaceutical industry, were approached. In agreeing to contribute to this book each person has contributed a high quality chapter and has helped to put together what is a unique book on cleaning and disinfection. The book is subtitled "a handbook" and this is the operative word that the editor would most like to see applied. This is not a book intended to sit on a shelf and gather dust, it is a book intended to be read and discussed by those tasked with the very important task of keeping cleanrooms, hospitals and the hands of staff, clean. If "The CDC Book" becomes an established part of the educational resources available to the workforce who aim to keep critical areas clean then the aims and intentions which shaped this book will have been a success.

The first edition of this book, issued in 2012, proved to be very popular and received positive feedback. Based on a need to update the text, in the context of changing standards and developments in the field, this second edition was produced. The central aim remains unchanged: to advise and to educate.

The editor welcomes any comments or clarifications in relation to the book and can be contacted at timsandle@btinternet.com

CHAPTER 1:

CLEANING AND DISINFECTION

By Tim Sandle

1.1 Introduction

Cleaning and disinfection practices are an essential part of contamination control in healthcare and in the pharmaceutical industry. These practices can be divided into two key parts:

- Cleaning and disinfection of cleanrooms, and
- Cleaning of equipment (which requires cleaning validation to verify the effectiveness of the cleaning)

The focus of this chapter, and indeed this book, is on the cleaning and disinfection of cleanrooms.

An important step towards achieving microbial control within a cleanroom is the use of defined cleaning techniques, together with the application of detergents and disinfectants. The objective of cleaning and disinfection is to achieve appropriate microbiological cleanliness levels for the class of cleanroom for an appropriate period of time. Thus the cleaning and disinfection of cleanrooms is an important part of contamination control (1).

This chapter examines both detergents (which 'clean') and disinfectants (which remove or eliminate microorganisms). Detergents are cleaning agents and are deployed to remove 'soil' from a surface. The removal of soil is an important step prior to the application of a disinfectant, for the greater the degree of soiling remaining on a surface, then the lesser the effectiveness of disinfection. A disinfectant is a type of chemical germicide which is capable of eliminating a population of vegetative microorganisms (although some disinfectants are sporicidal, a chemical does not need to be sporicidal to be classified as a disinfectant). A disinfectant which can kill spores is sometimes described as a sterilant or chemosterilant [(2)]. Disinfectants, of varying formulations, have been used since the late nineteenth century (3).

Disinfectants vary in their effectiveness against different types of microorganisms, a variation relating to both the intrinsic resistance of different microorganisms and the range of different types and formulations of disinfectants. Furthermore, different disinfectants act in different ways depending upon their active ingredients.

This chapter provides an introduction to cleaning and disinfection concepts and acts as a point of reference for the other chapters in this book.

The chapter is concerned with:

- The principles and definitions of cleaning, detergents and disinfectants.

- Introduction to the basic concepts relating to disinfection: contact time, mechanisms of action, spectrum of activity and resistance.
- The types of detergents and disinfectants commonly used.
- Outlining the important criteria for the selection of disinfectants.

1.2 Cleaning

Cleaning is the process of removing residues and 'soil' (such as dirt, grease, protein residues and so on) from surfaces to the extent that they are visually clean. This involves defined methods of application and often the use of a detergent. Importantly, the act of cleaning is necessary prior to the application of a disinfectant. A surface needs to be properly cleaned before the application of a disinfectant in order for the disinfectant to work efficiently (4), as disinfectants can either be inactivated by organic residues or the soil can create a barrier which prevents the disinfectant from reaching all of the microbial cells.

Whilst "cleaning" is not "disinfection" the cleaning process can remove or dilute microbial populations. Furthermore, many detergents have chemical additives that can 'disinfect'. However, a cleaning agent will not meet the criteria for disinfection required by the European and United States standards for disinfectant validation in terms of reducing a microbial population of a defined range by the required log reduction.

1.3 Detergents

What are detergents?

A detergent is a chemical used to clean equipment or surfaces by removing unwanted matter (soil). Detergents generally work by penetrating soil and reducing the surface tension (which adhere soil to the surface) to allow its removal (in crude terms, a detergent increases the 'wettability' of water). Many detergents are synthetic surfactants (an acronym for Surface Active Agents).

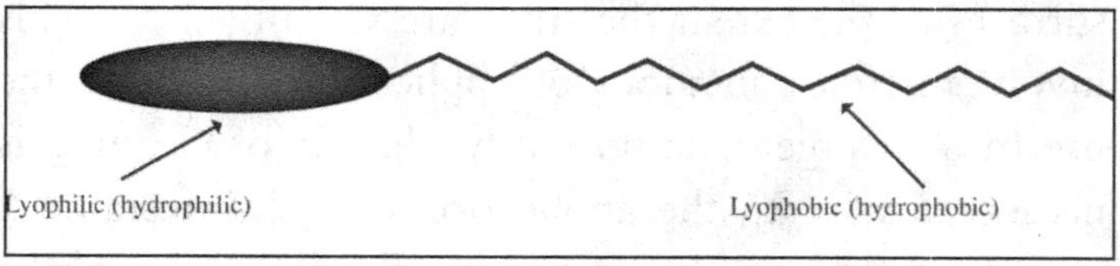

Figure 1: Simple schematic of a surfactant (© Licensed under Creative Commons)

Surfactants are schizophrenic molecules that have two sides to their nature. One part is solvent-loving or lyophilic (hydrophilic) and another is solvent-hating or lyophobic (hydrophobic). Surfactants remove particles from surfaces by either capillary effects or electrostatic forces (many detergents contain differently charged ions that can cause microorganisms to repel each other). This repulsion causes the microorganisms to disassociate from the surface and become suspended. Suspended microorganisms are easier to remove from the surface by the rinsing effect of the detergent (or a subsequent water rinse) or to be destroyed by the application of a disinfectant (5). The relative ease of killing microorganisms in planktonic state compared with killing microorganisms in the sessile state is reflected in the phased approach to disinfectant validation studies, as outlined in Chapter Ten (planktonic bacteria are free floating organisms; sessile bacteria are attached to a surface).

Selecting detergents

There are two key considerations when selecting detergents:

1) The chemical composition of the detergent.

With the chemical nature of the detergent, it is typical that detergents are neutral and non-ionic solutions. Furthermore, it is preferred that the detergents used are low- or non-foaming.

2) The compatibility of the detergent with the disinfectant.

In terms of compatibility, it is important that any detergent used should be compatible with the disinfectants used, for some detergents can leave residues which can neutralise the active ingredient in certain disinfectants thereby reducing the microcidal properties of the disinfectant (6).

There are various types of detergents, each with differing modes of cleansing action. In addition to cleansing action, some detergents have additional anti-microbial properties due to their ionic nature (anionic: negatively charged, or cationic: positively charged). Some examples of commonly used detergents are:

a) Soaps
b) Anionic detergents
c) Cationic detergents
d) Non-ionic detergents (or neutral detergents)
e) Amphoteric detergents (which have some bactericidal properties).
f) Alkali detergents
g) Acidic detergents

Additional chemicals are sometimes added to detergents to enhance their performance. Such additives include chemicals, which act to disperse fat and to produce uniform wetting, and sequestrants, which act against hard water and scaling.

Of the list of detergents, non-ionic detergents are the most commonly used in healthcare and pharmaceuticals. This is because such detergents are compatible with most commercial disinfectants; they are also useful for cleaning sensitive substrates due to their mild pH and enhanced compatibility. An alternative are the anionic detergents, such as sodium alkbenzine sulfonates (although these are often foam producing emulsifiers, which is not often desirable in cleanrooms); and cationic detergents like quaternary ammonium compounds. Acid and alkali detergents tend to be used for equipment processing, with alkali better for organic soils and acidic detergents better for inorganic soils.

1.4 Disinfection

Terminology

A disinfectant is a chemical agent, one of a very diverse group of products, which reduces the number of microorganisms present either by removing or destroying them. In literature various terms are applied in relation to this activity: disinfectant, antiseptic, asepsis and sanitiser.

The term disinfection is normally applied to an inanimate object (sometimes the term biocide is used, although this relates to a larger group of chemical agents). The term antiseptic is used to describe the reduction of a microbial population on living tissue (7). Thus an antiseptic is a disinfectant which can safely be applied to the surface of the skin[1] (8) (sometimes the terms 'hand sanitiser' or 'hand disinfectant' are used interchangeably.) In turn, the term disinfectant is usually reserved for liquid chemical germicides which cannot be applied to tissues because of their corrosive or toxic nature (9).

Asepsis can relate to the use of disinfectants to disinfect an area such as an operating theatre (and the term is more commonly associated with healthcare) (10). It is a separate term to 'aseptic technique', which, in the laboratory sense, relates to avoiding personnel contamination of devices intended to be sterile (11).

The term sanitiser is open to different interpretations. Within Europe, it is normally taken to be an agent that both cleans and disinfects (normally a disinfectant that contains a cleaning agent). Within North America (defined by the U.S. Environmental Protection Agency), however, the term is normally applied to an antimicrobial agent for use on non-food contact surfaces. Sanitisation is a general description for reducing a microbial population. Disinfection is a more precise term, as it can be related to the requirements of international standards in relation to the requirement that the chemical agent must reduce

[1] The term antisepsis is the use of chemicals as disinfection agents on the skin surface.

a known number of microorganisms (a property demonstrated through validation).

It is important to note that not all disinfectants are sporicidal. Sometimes the term 'sporicide' is used to differentiate this class of disinfectant.

1.5 Disinfectant efficacy

There are a number of important criteria which affect the performance and efficacy of disinfectants. These factors are:

i) Concentration

Disinfectants are manufactured or validated to be most efficacious at a set concentration range (the proportion of the chemical to water). The setting of this concentration range involves ascertaining the minimum inhibitory concentration (MIC). The MIC is the lowest concentration of the disinfectant that is shown to be bacteriostatic or bactericidal under experimental conditions. Experimental conditions are normally based on the examination of a disinfectant solution in suspension in the absence of soil. The MIC is measured through kinetic studies of the dilution coefficient. Kinetic studies demonstrate the effect of a change in concentration against cell death rate over time. The higher a disinfectant's concentration exponent, the longer it takes to kill cells. For example, if a disinfectant with a set concentration exponent was diluted by a factor of 2, the time taken for it to kill cells comparatively would double (12). The MIC is normally set by the manufacturer of the disinfectant.

ii) Time.

Time is an important factor in the application of disinfectants for two reasons: in relation to the contact time of the disinfectant and the expiry time of the disinfectant solution. Contact time (sometimes called the dwell time) is the time taken for the disinfectant to bind to the microorganism, traverse the cell wall and to reach the specific target site for the disinfectant's particular mode of action. Many disinfectants work best and meet product label claims when allowed to work for several minutes before wiping or rinsing.

Contact time relates to the concentration of the disinfectant (variation to the concentration of a disinfectant may alter the contact time required). In practical situations there are many variables which can alter the contact time. These include the type, concentration and volume of the disinfectant; the nature of the microorganisms; the amount and type of material present that is likely to interfere with the active ingredient; the temperature of the disinfectant; and the surface that the disinfectant is applied to.

Another aspect relating to time is the deterioration of a disinfectant solution over time. This is more important where a solution of disinfectant is prepared 'in-house' from a concentrate than to ready-prepared solutions, which have been validated by the manufacturer and will come with an assigned expiration time. For ready-prepared solutions, an expiry time limit for the disinfectant solution should be established through chemical testing. As a rule, fresh solutions of a disinfectant should be used for each application and between cleanrooms.

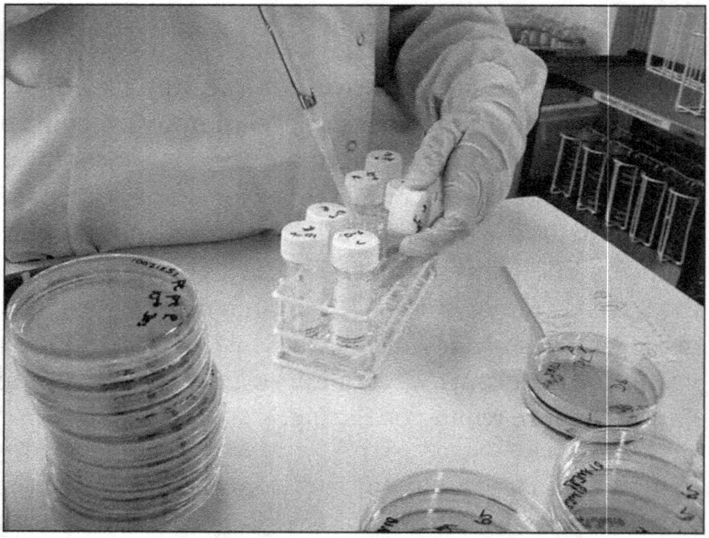

Figure 2: testing disinfectant samples in order to assess antimicrobial efficacy (© Tim Sandle)

iii) Number, type and location of microorganisms

Different species of microorganisms vary in their resistance to different disinfectants. These can be affected by: the numbers of microorganisms present, their species and the community with which they are bound to.

a) Number

An antimicrobial agent, like a disinfectant, is considerably more effective against a low number of microorganisms than a higher number or a population with a greater cell density. Similarly a disinfectant is more effective against a pure population than mixed grouping of microorganisms. A routine disinfectant procedure will be unlikely to kill all microorganisms present and a number will remain viable. Whether the surviving microorganisms multiply in sufficient number is dependent upon the condition in which the surviving population remains, the available nutrients and the time between repeat applications of the disinfectant.

b) Type of microorganism and resistance

Different types of microorganism have varying levels of resistance to broad spectrum disinfectants as Figure 3, below, shows. The increased resistance shown is primarily due to the cell membrane composition or type of protein coat.

The hierarchy of microorganisms in Figure 3 are placed in order of resistance. Resistance is either due to the natural genetic properties of the microorganisms

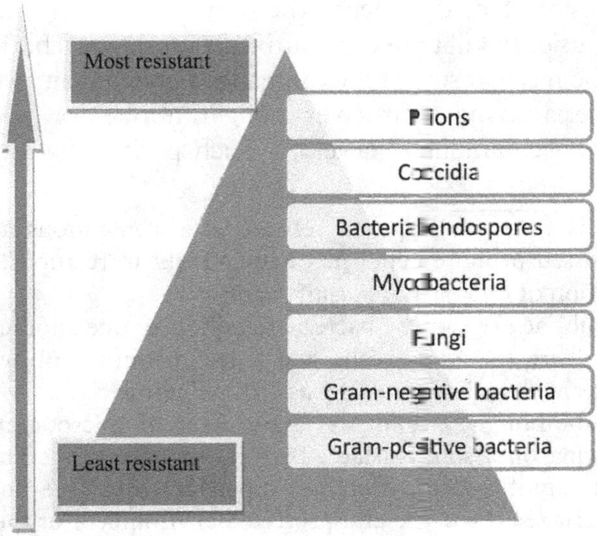

Figure 3: Sensitivity of different microorganisms to broad spectrum disinfectants (© Tim Sandle)

(intrinsic), as shown in Figure 3, or it is acquired through phenotypic (organism's actual observed properties, such as colony pigment) or genotypic (genetic) variations (similar to antibiotic resistance, through the over-use of one type of disinfectant[2]). Generally innate sensitivity results in Gram-negative bacteria being more resistant to disinfectant applications than Gram-positive bacteria, based on the composition of their cell wall. Fungi are the next least resistant (although some fungi can release enzymes which can inactivate some disinfectants); mycobacteria are next, having a level of resistance due to a waxy outer cell wall. In turn, for bacteria, endospores are the most resistant because of the relative impermeability of the spore coat.

c) Location of microorganisms

The location of microorganisms influences the effectiveness of disinfectant treatment. Microorganisms in suspension are easier to kill than those affixed to surfaces. This is due to the mechanisms of microorganism attachment, such as bacteria fixing themselves using fimbriae[3] or when a biofilm community[4] develops. Such positioning impacts

[2] This form of 'acquired resistance' is contentious and is discussed in more detail in Chapter Eight in relation to the rotation of two or more disinfectants.

[3] Fimbriae are used by bacteria to adhere to one another and to adhere to animal cells and some inanimate objects. A bacterium can have as many as 1,000 fimbriae.

[4] A biofilm is a complex aggregation of microorganisms growing on a solid surface. Bacteria living in a biofilm can have significantly different properties from free-floating bacteria, as the dense and protected environment of the film means that they have increased resistance to detergents and antibiotics, as the dense extracellular matrix and the outer layer of cells protect the interior of the community.

upon the contact time required for the disinfectant to bind to the microorganism, cross the cell wall and act at the required site. This is why, with disinfectant validation (see Chapter Ten), the surface test is regarded as more meaningful and robust than the suspension test.

iv) Temperature and pH

Each disinfectant has an optimal pH and temperature at which it is most effective. If the temperature or pH are outside this optimal range then the rate of reaction (log kill over time) is affected.

Temperature influences the rate of reaction. Most disinfectants are more effective and kill a population faster at higher temperatures although many disinfectants, due to practical considerations relating to cleanroom use, are manufactured to be used at ambient conditions. Disinfectants which are sensitive to temperatures other than at ambient are normally assessed through the use of a temperature coefficient, or Q_{10} (which relates the increase in activity to a 10°C rise in temperature) (13).

The effect of pH is important because it influences the ionic binding of a disinfectant to a bacterial cell wall thereby ensuring disinfectant molecules are bound to a high number of microorganisms. Many disinfectants are more stable at a set pH range. The use of a disinfectant outside of its desired pH range results in reduced efficacy.

v) Interfering substances

The presence of different substances on the surface or in the equipment requiring disinfection can affect the efficacy of the disinfectant in various ways ranging from increasing the contact time to complete inactivation. In order for a disinfectant to be effective it must come into contact with the microbial cell and be absorbed into it. If substances (or organic load), such as oil, dirt, blood serum, protein, food, body waste, paper or grease, act as a barrier between the microbial cell and the disinfectant, the efficacy of the disinfectant will be adversely affected. The presence of such substances (soil) halts disinfectant efficacy by either reacting with the disinfectant or creating a barrier for the disinfectant. This effect is increased if the surface itself has defects and crevices which limit disinfectant penetration (14). When purchasing disinfectants it is important to note if the label claim indicates if the disinfectant remains effective in the presence of small amounts of organic matter.

vi) Water

Many disinfectants do not work well in hard water. For use in the pharmaceutical and healthcare sectors, disinfectants are normally prepared using deionised or demineralised water (or Water for Injections in the higher grade cleanrooms).

1.6 Types of disinfectants

There are various types of disinfectants available (in 2012 over 8,000 disinfectant products were registered with the U.S. Environmental Protection Agency (EPA) alone). Different types of disinfectants have different spectra of activity, modes of action and differing efficacies. Some disinfectants are classed as *bacteriostatic*, where the ability of the bacterial population to grow is halted. Here the disinfectant can cause selective and reversible changes to cells by interacting with nucleic acids, inhibiting enzymes or permeating into the cell wall. Once the disinfectant is removed from contact with bacteria cells, the surviving bacterial population could potentially grow.

Other disinfectants are *bactericidal* in that they destroy bacterial cells through different mechanisms. These include: causing structural damage to the cell, autolysis, cell lysis, or by the leakage or coagulation of the cytoplasm. Within these groups, the spectrum of activity varies, with some disinfectants being effective against vegetative Gram-positive and Gram-negative microorganisms only, while other disinfectants are effective against fungi. Other disinfectants have a broader spectrum and are sporicidal in that they can cause the destruction of endospore forming bacteria. However, a chemical agent does not have to be sporicidal in order to be classed as a 'disinfectant' (15). The bacteriostatic, bactericidal and sporicidal properties of a disinfectant are influenced by many variables. These variables are examined later.

There are a number of disinfectants available in the market with different modes of activity and of varying effectiveness against microorganisms. There are various approaches to the categorisation and sub-division of disinfectants including grouping by chemical nature, mode of activity or by microstatic and microcidal effects on microorganisms. This chapter discusses some of the more commonly used disinfectants employed in the healthcare and pharmaceutical environments by categorising them according to their chemical properties. The two principal categories used are the division into oxidising and non-oxidising chemicals. The reader should note that the list below is not exhaustive.

Non-oxidising disinfectants

The majority of this group of disinfectants have specific modes of action against microorganisms but generally they have a lower spectrum of activity compared to oxidising disinfectants (16). The most common types of non-oxidising disinfectants are alcohols, quaternary ammonium compounds and phenolics.

i) Alcohols

Alcohols have an antibacterial action against vegetative cells. The effectiveness of alcohols against vegetative bacteria and fungi increases with their molecular weight (therefore ethanol is more effective than methanol and in turn isopropyl alcohols more effective than ethanol) (17). Alcohols, where efficacy is increased with the presence of water, act on the bacterial cell wall by making it permeable. This can result in cytoplasm leakage, denaturation of protein and eventual cell lysis. The advantages of employing alcohols include a relatively low cost, little odour and a quick evaporation. Furthermore alcohols have a partial cleansing action (18).

ii) Aldehydes

Aldehydes include long chain chemical compounds, such as formaldehyde and gluteraldehyde. Aldehydes have a wide spectrum of activity and a non-specific effect in the denaturation of bacterial cell proteins and can cause coagulation of cellular protein. Certain aldehydes, such as glutaldehyde are rarely used today due to health and safety concerns (19).

iii) Amphoterics

Amphoterics are acidic, having a relatively wide spectrum of activity, but are limited by their ability to damage endospores. Amphoterics are frequently used as surface disinfectants. An example is alkyl di(aminoethyl) glycine or derivatives (20).

iv) Acid anionics

Acid anionics (such as sodium lauryl sulphate) are weak acids with a relatively limited spectrum of activity and are very pH dependent. An example of this group is carboxylic acid. They are not effective against fungi or spore forming bacteria. Their bactericidal properties arise from their ability to cause bacterial cell disruption which affects cellular division (21).

v) Biguanides

Biguanides are polymers supplied in salt form, such as chlorhexidine, alexidine or hydrochloride. Biguanides have a relatively wide spectrum of activity with the exception of killing endospores. Biguanides work best on surfaces which are at an alkaline or neutral pH. They are less effective under acidic conditions. Biguanides affect the bacterial cell membrane, enter the cell through diffusion, and cause cell disruption and cytoplasm leakage (22).

vi) Phenolics

Phenols are produced from the fractionation of tar and are among the oldest scientifically evaluated disinfectants dating back to Robert Koch's evaluation of phenol's bactericidal effect against *Bacillus anthraci* and Lister's application of phenol in hospital surgery units. The commonly used phenolic is basic phenol (carbolic acid) although synthetic variants are being widely used. Phenol can be made more complex by the addition of halogens such as chlorine (the bis-phenols and halophenols), to the phenol molecule (carbolic acid), to make compounds like triclosan and chloroxylenol. Phenols are bactericidal, and antifungal, but are not effective against spores (23).

Anionic surfactants are added to many phenolic disinfectants to provide a degree of cleaning ability and tend to be more efficient as an acidic formulation (24). Care must be taken to ensure that residues of phenolics are removed if phenolics are used in rotation with Quaternary ammonium chloride products, which are cationic in nature, as the two disinfectants are chemically incompatible.

vii) Quaternary ammonium compounds (QACs)

QACs are cationic salts of organically substituted ammonium compounds and have a fairly broad range of activity against microorganisms, albeit more effective against Gram-positive bacterium at lower concentrations than Gram-negative bacteria. They are considerably less effective against spore formers.

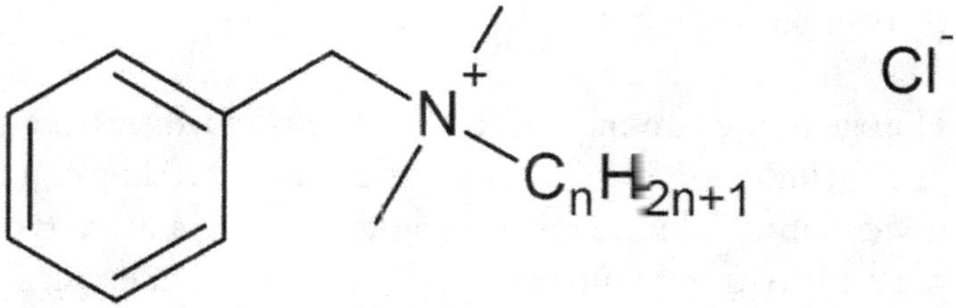

$$n = 8, 10, 12, 14, 16, 18$$

Figure 4: Formula of a common QAC: benzalkonium chloride (© Tim Sandle)

QACs are sometimes classified as surfactants and are available in both alkali and acidic formulations. An example is benzalkonium chloride. QACs are the most widely used of the non-oxidising disinfectants within the pharmaceutical industry. Their mode of action is on the cell membrane leading to cytoplasm leakage and cytoplasm coagulation through interaction with phospholipids. As the disinfectant carries a positive charge it is attracted to the negatively charged bacterial cell wall, thereby leading to the absorption of the chemical (25).

Oxidising disinfectants

This group of disinfectants generally have non-specific modes of action against microorganisms. They have a wider spectrum of activity than non-oxidising disinfectants, with most types able to damage endospores, but they pose greater risks to human health.

i) Halogens

Halogens are among the oldest identified disinfectants and include organic and inorganic varieties. They can be divided into chlorine releasing and iodophors. Both types have a broad spectrum of activity against a wide range of microorganisms and are normally effective sporicides (26). Examples of chlorine releasing chemicals are sodium trichloroisocyanurate, sodium hypochlorite (bleach) and chlorinated trisodium phosphonate. Hypochlorites are one of the oldest commercial disinfectants. The mode of action of this group is not completely known. One concern with using such agents is the damage that they can cause to cleanroom surfaces through corrosion, especially at high concentrations (>1000 parts per million). Such chemicals can also be respiratory irritants.

The most commonly used disinfectant in this group is chlorine dioxide. This disinfectant is normally produced as a two-component system (sodium chlorite and an organic acid like lactic acid). Chlorine dioxide is generated when the base (sodium chlorite) reacts with the activator (the organic acid). The shelf-life of the solution is normally fairly limited.

Iodine is another disinfectant with a long history. Most commercial iodine based disinfectants consist of iodine formulated with surfactants or polymers in an acidic solution. The effectiveness of iodine disinfectants is determined by the amount of free I_2. Iodine acts by iodinating tyrosine residues in cells. The disadvantage of iodine is its ability to stain and it also gives an unpleasant odour.

ii) Oxidising agents

This group includes oxygen releasing compounds like peracetic acid and hydrogen peroxide. They are often used in the gaseous phase as surface sterilants for equipment. These peroxygens function by disrupting the cell wall causing cytoplasm leakage and they denature bacterial cell enzymes through oxidation (from a powerful hydroxyl radical). These oxidising agents have advantages in that they are clear and colourless, thereby avoiding staining, but they do present some health and safety concerns particularly in terms of causing respiratory difficulties to unprotected users.

Hydrogen peroxide is a commonly used disinfectant, partly because of it having a low level of corrosiveness to surface metals and because it degrades to water and oxygen (and therefore leaves minimum residue). Hydrogen peroxide is used at a concentration range of 3%-10%. Peracetic acid is formed from the combination of hydrogen peroxide and acetic acid, where the reaction creates the oxidising agent. It will sometimes leave a residue on surfaces and has a pungent odour, and its use is more confined to gassing or fogging systems (27).

1.7 Selecting disinfectants

Deciding the types of disinfectants to be used in cleanrooms is an important decision for cleanroom managers. When selecting disinfectants, there are a number of different criteria to consider. These criteria are examined below (28).

A disinfectant must have a wide spectrum of activity.

The spectrum of activity refers to the properties of a disinfectant being effective against a wide range of vegetative microorganisms including Gram-negative and Gram-positive bacteria. For use in cleanrooms, disinfectants should be bactericidal (that is rather than simply inhibiting microbial growth, it should be capable of killing bacteria). A separate decision to be made is whether the disinfectant is required to be sporicidal. Furthermore in some facilities the disinfectants should also be virucidal.

A disinfectant should have a fairly rapid action.

The speed of action depends upon the contact time required for the disinfectant to destroy a microbial population. Thus the 'minimum' contact time is the time required for the disinfectant to be effective after its application. The contact time is sometimes referred to as the 'action time' or 'dwell time'. Given the requirements of most pharmaceutical manufacturers and healthcare facilities a disinfectant should ideally have a contact time of 10 minutes or less, although certain sporicidal disinfectants can require longer contact times.

Disinfectants should not be neutralised by residual matter

Although detergents and effective cleaning practices can remove the majority of soil, including organic matter, some traces will remain. It is important these organic residues do not interfere with the active ingredient of the disinfectant and reduce its efficacy.

Environmental conditions

Some disinfectants require certain temperatures and pH ranges in order to function properly. One type of disinfectant, for example, may not be effective in a cold room due to the lower temperature. The reason for this is the validation standards for disinfectants measure the bactericidal activity at 20°C; therefore the disinfectant may not be as effective at higher or lower temperatures.

Non-corrosive

Disinfectants should be non-corrosive. If the disinfectant causes extensive abrasion of a surface, it will either degrade the material or cause cracks and recesses which can harbour microorganisms. It is recognised, however, that the most efficacious disinfectants, especially those which are sporicidal, through repeated applications over time will cause some corrosion. A post-disinfection step to remove disinfectant residues, such as a sterile water rinse or wiping with a milder disinfectant like 70% IPA, can minimise material surface damage.

Operator safety

Many disinfectants are toxic or irritant and unpleasant for staff to use. Consideration must be given to safety requirements, material safety data sheets, label information, the toxicity upon human health and to the protective measures required for staff to use them (such as avoiding contact with exposed skin or the need to use a disinfectant in a well-ventilated area).

Compatibility with the surface to be disinfected

Some disinfectants may be less effective with certain materials or may cause excessive damage to certain materials, such as the reaction of chlorine dioxide against stainless steel.

Compatibility with detergents used

As discussed above, it is important that the disinfectant and detergent are compatible and that detergent residues do not inactivate the active ingredients in the disinfectant solution.

Residual activity of the disinfectant

Residual activity of the disinfectant may lead to resistant strains or cause problems when an alternative disinfectant is applied. It is good practice to remove disinfectant residues with a water rinse.

Sporicidal properties

If isolates from the environmental monitoring programme include the recovery of endospore forming bacteria on a frequent basis or in high numbers, then the use of a sporicidal disinfectant is essential, with the frequency determined by a review of the environmental monitoring programme.

Range of formats available.

The cleanroom facility will require a disinfectant to be available in several formats (29). For example a type and

Figure 5: Environmental monitoring samples (© Tim Sandle)

formulation of disinfectant may be required in a ready-to-use format, as a concentrate, or an impregnated wipe, and so on, so that the most convenient and effective method of cleaning can be used. The pharmaceutical manufacturer, when selecting cleaning agents, should aim for products which are produced in different presentations. For smaller spillages and the cleaning of process area surfaces and laboratory benches, sterile disinfectants in trigger sprays are the most effective design. With slightly larger areas, ready-to-use disinfectant solutions in bigger volumes are desirable. For cleaning larger areas, such as process area floors, it is more practical and cost effective for disinfectants to be supplied in the concentrate form (for this the disinfectant is prepared by cleanroom operators by dilution).

Cost

The calculation of cost needs to include not just the price of the disinfectant, but also other cost factors such as the time taken to prepare or apply the disinfectant, protective clothing requirements, wastage and the steps needed for the removal of residues.

Health and safety

The safety aspects of a disinfectant are an important consideration. Standard operating procedures should contain appropriate health and safety requirements for using detergents and disinfectants. This should include reference to appropriate personal protective equipment. In particular, contact to eyes, skin and mouth is to be avoided. Safety data sheets must be examined for all disinfectants and detergents and appropriate measures taken to ensure that they are applied properly, in well-ventilated areas.

1.8 Summary

In order to achieve microbial control in cleanrooms, the use of defined cleaning techniques together with the application of detergents and disinfectants, is of great importance (30). This chapter has examined the basics of cleaning and disinfection and has outlined the key terms relating to detergents and disinfectants. The chapter has summarised the main types of disinfectants available and explained some of the key terms which need to be understood when considering disinfectant efficacy. The chapter has also presented some of the important factors to consider when selecting a disinfectant for use within a cleanroom.

Selecting appropriate detergents and disinfectants is an important choice for the cleanroom manager and the microbiologist to make. The performance of the agents selected should be regularly reviewed, drawing on important information including the results of microbiological environmental monitoring.

1.9 References

1. Sutton, S.V.W. 'Disinfectant Rotation in a Cleaning / Disinfection Program for Cleanrooms and Controlled Environments', in Manivannan, G. (Ed.), *Disinfection and Decontamination: Principles, Applications and Related Issues*, CRC Press 2008, pp165-174
2. Gorman, S. and Scott, E. 'Chemical disinfectants, antiseptics and preservatives' in Denyer, S.P., Hodges, N.A. and Gorman, S.P. *Hugo and Russell's Pharmaceutical Microbiology*, 7th Edition, 2004, Oxford: Blackwell, pp285-305
3. Worboys, M. 'Public and Environmental Health' in Bowler, P.J. and Pickstone. J.V. (Eds.) *The Cambridge History of Science Vol. 6.: The Modern Biological and Earth Sciences*, Cambridge: Cambridge University Press, 2009.
4. Bessems, E.: 'The effect of practical conditions on the efficacy of disinfectants', *International Biodeterioration and Biodegradation*, 41, 1998, pp177-183
5. Farn, R.J. *Chemistry and technology of surfactants*, London: John Wiley & Sons, 2006.
6. Collier, L., Balows, A. and Sussman, M. (1998): *Topley and Wilson's Microbiology and Microbial Infections Volume 2: Systematic Bacteriology*, Ninth Edition, 1998 New York: Arnold, pp149-170
7. Marcovitch, H. *Black's Medical Dictionary*, 42nd Edition, London: A&C Black, 2010, p193.
8. Taylor, D.J., Green, N.P.O. and Stout, G.W. *Biological Science 2: Systems, Maintenance and*

Change, Third Edition, Cambridge: Cambridge University Press, 1997.

9. Brooker, C. (Ed.) *Mosby's Dictionary of Medicine, Nursing and Healthcare Professions*. Elsevier: Edinburgh, 2010.
10. Gariepy, T.J. 'Antisepsis' in Heilbron, J.L. (Ed.) *The Oxford Companion to the History of Modern Science*, Oxford: Oxford University Press, 2003.
11. Wilson J. *Infection Control in Clinical Practice*, 2nd Edition, Bailliere Tindall: London, 2006.
12. Russell, A. D.: 'Assessment of sporicidal efficacy', *International Biodeterioration and Biodegradation*, 41, 1998, pp281-287
13. Cooper, M.S.: 'Biocides and Preservatives', *The Microbiological Update*, June 2000, Vol. 18, No.3, pp1-4
14. Frank, J.F. and Chmielewski, R. (2001): 'Influence of Surface Finish on the Cleanability of Stainless Steel', *Journal of Food Protection*, Vol. 64, No.8, pp1178-1182
15. O'Leary, W.M. *Practical Handbook of Microbiology*, 1977, second edition, CRC Press, Florida, USA
16. Denyer, S.P. and Stewart, G.S.A.B.: 'Mechanisms of action of disinfectants', *International Biodeteriroration and Biodegradation*, 41, 1998, pp261-268
17. Considine, G.D. and Kulik, P. H. *Van Nostrad's Scientific Encyclopaedia*, 10th Edition. New Jersey: Wiley-Interscience, 2008.
18. McDonnell, G. and Russell, A.: 'Antiseptics and Disinfectants: Activity, Action and Resistance', *Clinical Microbiology Reviews*, Jan. 1999, pp147-179

19. Angelillo, I.F., Bianco, A., Nobile, C.G.A. and Pavia, M.: 'Evaluation of the efficacy of glutaraldehyde and peroxygen for disinfection of dental instruments', *Letters in Applied Microbiology*, 1998, 27, 292-296
20. Bluestein, B. R. and Hilton, C.L. *Amphoteric surfactants*, New York: M. Dekker, 1982
21. Rossmore, H. W. *Handbook of biocide and preservative use*, New York: Springer, 1995, p319
22. Kanegsberg, B. *Handbook for critical cleaning*, New York: CRC Press, 2011.
23. Bergan, T. and Lystad, A.: 'Evaluation of Disinfectant Inactivators', *Acta path. Microbiol.* Scand. Section B., 1972, 80, pp507 – 510
24. Connor, D. E. and Eckman, M. K. 'Rotation of phenolic disinfectants', *Pharm. Technol.*, September 1992, pp148-162
25. Block, S.S. *Disinfection, sterilization, and preservation*, Lippincott Williams & Wilkins: Philadelphia, 2001, p474
26. Pommerville, J.C. *Alcamo's Fundamentals of Microbiology*, Ninth Edition, Burlington, MA: Jones & Bartlett Learning, 2010, p208
27. Mendez-Vilas, A. *Current Research Topics in Applied Microbiology and Microbial Biotechnology: Proceedings of the II International Conference on Environmental, Industrial and Applied Microbiology (Biomicroworld2007)*, Singapore: World Scientific, 2009, p199
28. Morton, L.H.G., Greenway, D. L.A., Gaylarde, C.C. and Surman, S. B.: Consideration of some implications of resistance of biofilms to biocides, *International Biodeterioration and Biodegradation*, 41 (1998), pp247-259

29. Denyer, S.P. and Stewart, G.S.A.B.: 'Mechanisms of action of disinfectants', *International Biodeterироration and Biodegradation*, 41, 1998, pp261-268
30. Sandle, T.: 'Selection and use of cleaning and disinfection agents in pharmaceutical manufacturing' in Hodges, N and Hanlon, G. (2003): *Industrial Pharmaceutical Microbiology Standards and Controls*, Euromed Communications, England

CHAPTER 2:

HAND SANITISATION AND ANTISEPTICS

By Ian M. Jarvis

2.1 Introduction

In humans it is believed that approximately 80% of all micro-organisms are transferred by our hands and although the use of soap and water has historically been the best and most important first line of defence against transfer of bacterial contamination from person to person or from person to object it has its failings both, in terms effectiveness and where it can be successfully performed. Due to increased knowledge, new products and better appreciation of the risks associated with bacterial and viral infection there has been a revolution in the number and type of products available to both the homeowner and the health care industry.

There is always a balance to be struck with regards to hand sanitisation, based on the effectiveness of the agent and the integrity of the skin, both in terms of sensitising and damage. Harsh chemicals although effective against bacteria and viruses are not suitable for use on the skin and as such a compromise is always required. This balance is shifted if the user is wearing gloves however other factors then come into play.

The use of the term hand sanitisers and hand antiseptics are often used interchangeably to describe the same act of bacterial removal however there are differences. Sanitisers are substances that simultaneously clean and disinfect but have a short activity span in that the hands can easily become re-contaminated after touching a contaminated surface. Sanitisation is also a very broad umbrella term often used in describing the removal of bacteria on any surface, including the human body, but also inanimate surfaces, both of which demand very different types of sanitising agents. Hand antiseptics, however are designed specifically to destroy micro-organisms on living tissue and have a longer activity span in that they often bind to the surface of the skin and provide a higher degree of protection. Sanitising agents and antiseptics can also differ in their mode of action against the bacteria, again separating the two into distinct classes. To add to the confusion, hand sanitisers generally fall into two groups, alcohol based and non-alcohol based. The term hygienic handrub is commonly used to describe the alcohol based formulations and as the name suggests these products are designed to be applied by gentle rubbing over the surface of the hand, at the point of care.

The growth and development of microorganisms can be inhibited by the use of antiseptics which are routinely used in topical applications, such as skin application and on hard surfaces. A diverse range of antiseptics are used routinely in both, hospital, manufacturing and home environments. They are used for their anti-infective effects on bacteria, being either bactericidal and/or bacteriostatic and are used primarily for cleansing of wounds following trauma, preparation of surfaces prior to surgery, manufacturing or food preparation and cleaning of hands to prevent cross contamination. The type of antiseptic used and its concentration is very much dependant on its intended use, with common compounds such as benzalkonium chloride, chlorhexidine, methyl salicylate, hexachlorophine, iodine compounds and alcohol being widely used.

2.2 Skin Microflora

It is important that we try and distinguish between the different micro-organisms found on the skin before we seek to find methods for the removal and/or destruction of such micro-organisms. To help us it is useful to divide the microorganisms typically carried on the skin into two discrete populations (1, 2, 5), resident and transient. Resident microorganisms such as *Staphylococcus* species and *Micrococcus* species and *Corynebacteirum* (or 'diptheroids') are generally considered to be permanent inhabitants of the skin and are found primarily on the skin surface with a smaller number being found within the epidermal layer, where natural skin secretions and hardened skin make their removal challenging.

Transient microorganisms as the name suggests, are picked up from surfaces we touch or from aerosols carrying bacteria and reside exclusively on and within the epidermal (5) layer of the skin. A large proportion of these organisms can be pathogenic such as *Salmonella* spp., *Shigella* spp., *Escherichia coli*, *Clostridium perfringens*, yeasts, moulds and viruses. Each can lead to infections of the skin if the normal balance of residual microorganisms has been disturbed. This class of microflora are certainly not normal residents on the skin and they can pose a serious risk to health, especially in a hospital or pharmaceutical manufacturing environment or where food is prepared. The good news is that this transient population is virtually always removed by hand washing, using soap and mechanical friction or by the use of sanitising/antiseptic hand rubs.

However it should be noted that it is impossible to effectively remove all microflora from the skin be it transient or resident, even when using the most powerful sanitising agents or antiseptics. If something approaching sterile conditions are required then the use of sterile, disposable gloves is the only option.

2.3 Common Sanitisation/Antiseptic agents

2.3.1 Alcohols

Alcohol rubs are a useful alternative to soap and water when hand washing is impractical or not available.

Alcohols are widely used as sanitising agents with ethanol, n-propanol and isopropyl alcohol (IPA) widely used in aqueous solution and gel formulations (1). They are an effective antiseptic, non-corrosive, leave little residue if used in a pure solution with water and dry quickly, however there have been some reports that prolonged use of alcohol gels can lead to lipid barrier depletion within the skin surface over time. Pure alcohol containing hand sanitisers can cause irritant contact dermatitis with symptoms such as dryness of the skin, irritation and even cracking and bleeding to occur (11). In response to the concerns raised by the use of alcohols some suppliers include emollients and moisturisers within their formulations to help protect the skin. As a general rule, care should be taken in using moisturisers on their own after hand washing as they can form a barrier to the effectiveness of the alcohol and may not be compatible with the sanitisation agent being used.

Pure alcohols have limited effectiveness on the skin surface as they quickly evaporate which results in low contact times and penetration through the cell membrane of the micro-organism. Typically a mixture of 70% alcohol to 30% purified water is used, although this figure can vary especially in gel formulations. The addition of water helps to facilitate the diffusion through the membrane of the bacterial cell and improves the skin contact time by slowing down evaporation. Literature concerning alcohol effectiveness against bacteria does vary but in general it does conclude that it is effective against a wide spectrum of bacteria but has limited effect on viruses and no effect on bacterial and fungal spores (12).

2.3.2 Quaternary ammonium compounds

Some Quaternary ammonium compounds have been shown to have antimicrobial activity (2), such as benzalkonium chloride. Quarternary ammonium compounds, often referred to as "Quats" are a very large class of chemical compounds and are present in thousands of end use formulations, including disinfectants, surfactants and even fabric conditioners. Often used in combination with other Quats they can bind strongly to organic and inorganic surfaces due to their cationic nature. Benzalkonium chloride (BKC), is a very common Quat used in antiseptic preparations, it is stable chemically and has a long lasting biocidal effect, based on its ability to attach to the bacteria and cause the cytoplasmic membrane to leak, damaging and eventually killing the bacteria.

Often presented in combination with alcohols, BKC and similar compounds have a high degree of safety when applied in the correct concentration and serve as an effective broad-spectrum disinfectant.

2.3.3 Bisbiguanides

Chlorhexidine gluconate (CHG) is a common antiseptic found in a large number of antimicrobial preparations, both for topical and oral use it belongs to the chemical group known as biguanides.

Because of its cationic nature, chlorhexidine binds strongly to skin, mucosa and tissues and is thus very poorly absorbed by the body. CHG is effective against most microorganisms (2) but its effectiveness is very much dependent on the formulation and its concentration.

It is effective against a wide range of Gram negative and Gram positive vegetative bacteria, yeasts, dermatophyte fungi and lipophilic viruses. At low concentrations, CHG binds to the negatively charged cell wall and disrupts its osmotic equilibrium (1,9). At higher concentrations CHG attacks the bacterial cytoplasmic membrane and denatures microbial proteins. CHG has both a rapid onset of bactericidal action and prolonged antimicrobial efficacy through a residual antimicrobial film on the skin similar to benzalkonium chloride.

2.3.4 Povidone Iodine

Povidone-iodine is a stable chemical complex of polyvinylpyrrolidone and iodine (PVPI), typically containing 9 to 12% of available iodine and has become the universally preferred iodine antiseptic. Typically used for surgical hand scrubs and preparation of surgical sites it has the broadest spectrum of all topical anti-infectives, with action against bacteria, fungi, yeasts, viruses, protozoa and spores. The slow release of iodine from the PVPI complex in solution minimizes iodine toxicity towards human cells.

Aqueous solutions of iodine have also been used as antiseptic agents, but are less effective than alcoholic solutions and less convenient to use than the povidone iodine compounds.

2.4 Storage and Precautions

Sanitising and antiseptic cleaning agents should be stored, controlled and used in the correct manner, taking due regard of the manufactures recommendations (7). If incorrectly stored their effectiveness can be severely affected, especially if exposed to excessive heat/light or left exposed to the environment. On no account should antiseptics be transferred to alternative containers, diluted or mixed with other compounds, benzalkonium chloride for example is inactivated by organic compounds, including soap, therefore all residues of soap should be removed prior to using formulations containing this compound.

Dilution of cleaning agents not in accordance with manufacturer's instructions has been known to give rise to microbiological contamination, especially if the diluted formulation has been used or stored over a prolonged period of time or has been contaminated in some way. The quality of water used to make up dilutions as well as the container used also pose significant risks to the effectiveness of the solution.

2.5 Hand washing Techniques

Like all tasks there is often a right way and a wrong way to do something, the same is very much true for hand washing. Although hand washing is a very effective means of preventing cross contamination, if not carried out in a prescribed way it can be rendered useless. Imagine an individual taking time and effort in cleaning their hands thoroughly, only to be re-contaminated by the method they use to dry their hands e.g. the use of a dirty old hand towel.

Figure 1, the areas highlighted indicate the typical areas often missed by hand washing. The tips of the fingers, between the fingers and the back of the thumb tend to be missed due to poor technique and other areas on the hand are also frequently missed especially if the activity is rushed.

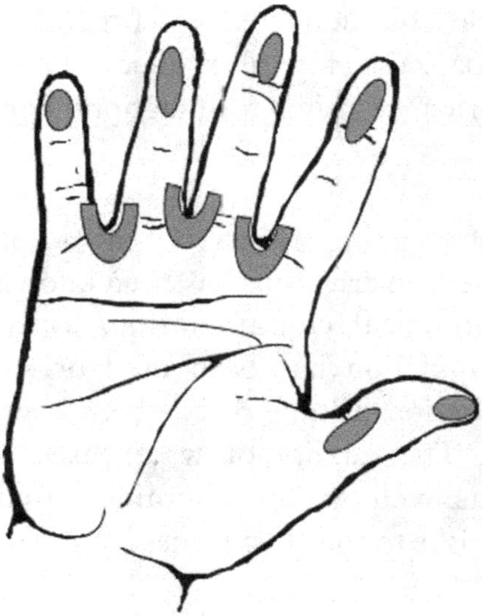

Figure 1. Areas often missed by hand washing

Ideally if the hands are soiled and before a sanitising/antiseptic agent is used, the hands should be thoroughly washed with soap and water for a minimum of 30 seconds, taking care to cover all parts of the hands in accordance with **Figure 2** (2). This removes approximately 95% of all the transient microorganisms, although this again depends on the residual dirt on the hands at the start of the process, as a rough guide the hands should be visibly clean. The act of rubbing the hands together is important in this procedure as it acts as a physical mechanism of bacterial removal, ensuring that dead skin is also removed which can hinder the action of any sanitising agent applied later. Hands should be thoroughly dried using disposable towels or hot air driers.

Pure soap, devoid of perfumes or other non-essential additives are preferred in order to reduce the potential for residues on the skin and possible interactions with sanitizing agents. If possible liquid soap should be used, which is presented in disposable clean packaging and keeps the area around the washing station hygienic.

A sanitising/antiseptic agent can then be applied in accordance with the manufacturers recommendations, it should be noted that it is important to follow these instructions carefully to maximise the effect of the solution or gel applied. The amount applied and contact time will vary as will drying time, but typically this will take no longer than 60 seconds.

Both sanitising and antiseptic agents are often presented in pump dispensers, squeezable bottles or pressurised containers and are typically designed to enable the user to activate the pump by pressing down with one hand or elbow whilst dispensing the agent into the palm of the other hand.

After application, the hands should be rubbed together gently in order to spread the solution evenly over both hands, paying particular attention to the fingers, thumbs, nails, wrists, palms, back of the hands and between the fingers. The process is described in **Figure 2**. Care should be taken not to use too much solution as apart from being wasteful, there is danger of spilling the solution from the hands onto the floor leading to a slip hazard.

Figure 2. Hand washing/Sanitising Steps

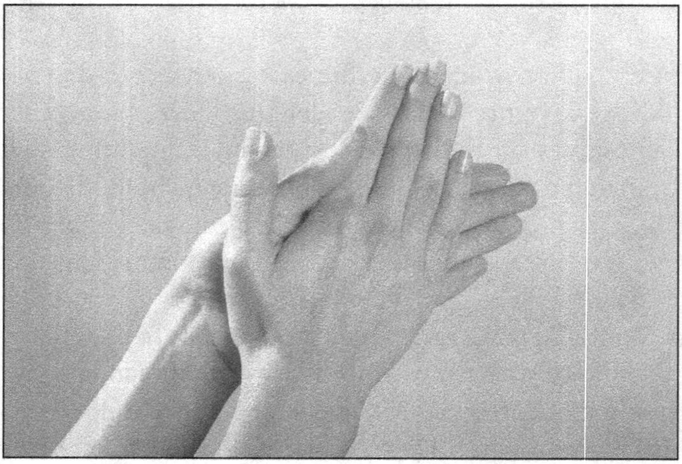

Figure 2.1 Following application of soap/sanitising/ antiseptic agent, rub the hands together palm to palm and rub each wrist with opposite hand.

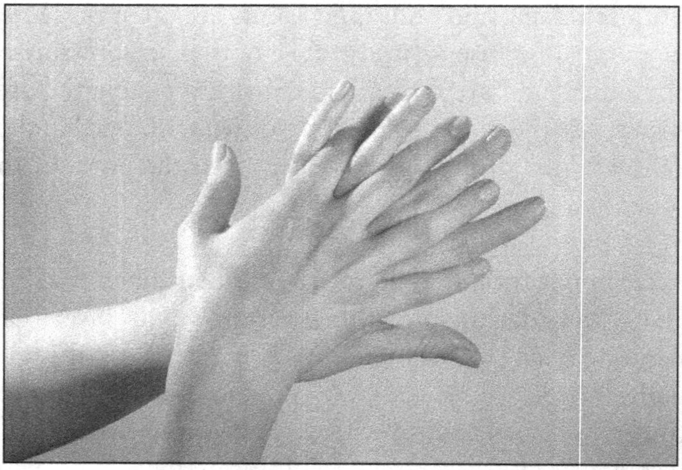

Figure 2.2 Rub the back of each hand with the palm of the other hand with fingers interlaced – and vice versa

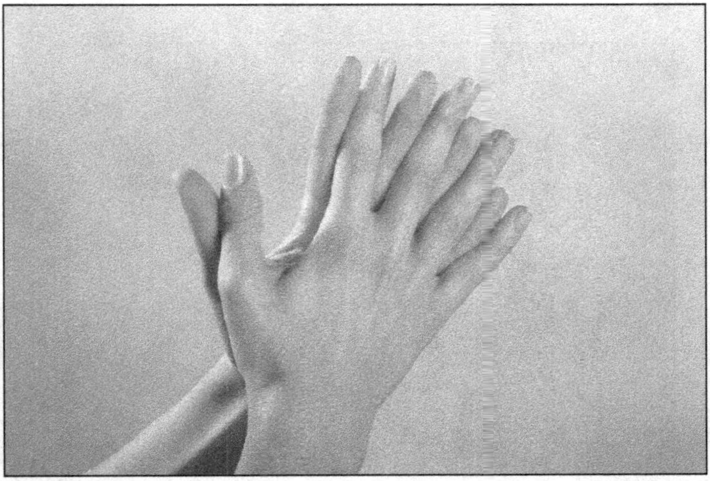

Figure 2.3 Rub palm to palm with interlaced spread fingers

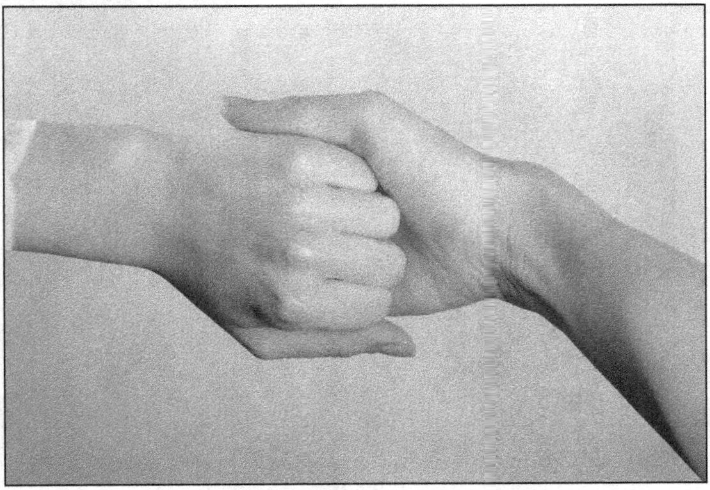

Figure 2.4 Rub the backs of the interlocked fingers on the opposing palms

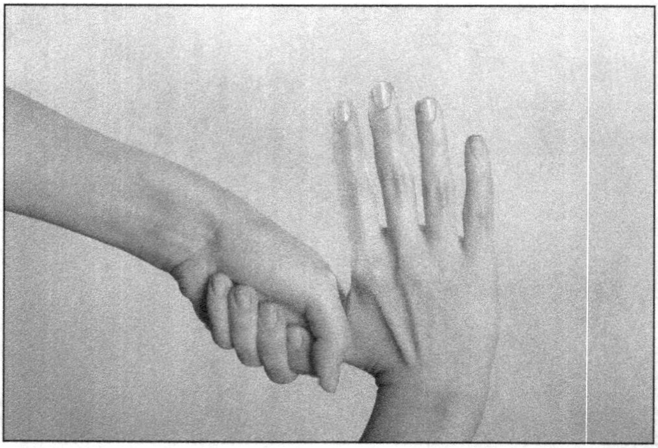

Figure 2.5 Rub the right thumb in the closed palm of the left hand using a circular motion, then repeat on the other hand.

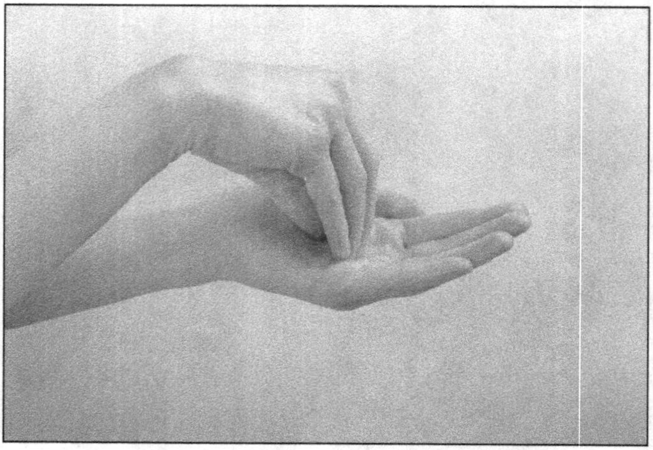

Figure 2.6 Rub the closed fingertips of the right hand on the left palm using a circular motion, and again repeat on the other hand.

Following this initial application regular hand disinfection should take place to eliminate any subsequent transient micro-organisms being picked up from other surfaces or contact with people and to reduce the risk of the contamination arising from resident skin flora. Given that alcohols are typically used in sanitising solutions/gels they do not afford continual antimicrobial action/protection due to their volatility. Simple tasks such as using door handles, touching spectacles, using a pen, picking up a phone will automatically re-introduce potentially pathogenic bacteria onto the skin. Therefore frequent re-sanitisation and hand washing is crucial in preventing cross contamination.

2.6 Hand Sanitisation in a Cleanroom Environment

The initial phase of hand washing for a cleanroom environment is very similar to that described for a normal hand washer protocol in **Figure 2**. However there are some differences and these often relate to the type of cleanroom or activity taking place within that environment, i.e. surgical, pharmaceutical etc. For the sake of clarity, this section will focus on the typical procedures involved in the preparation of aseptically prepared pharmaceuticals.

Each aseptic facility will have its own approved procedures relating to hand hygiene, gloving and contamination control based on experience and the type of challenges governed by the facility, the equipment used and formulation type (6,7).

What is common is that all jewellery and watches harbour bacteria and must be removed before any hand washing starts (7). Nails should be free from varnish and kept short to limit the build up of transient bacteria. On no account should false nails be worn as these not only are difficult to clean but also pose a significant risk to glove puncture and make any gloving process difficult.

Hands and forearms should be washed up to the elbows with a mild liquid soap, taking care to clean under finger nails. Sterile nail brushes if used, should be single use only and used on nails and not to scrub the skin as this can lead to skin damage over prolonged periods.

With the hands/arms dry, an antiseptic hand wash can be applied, typically a solution of chlorhexidine gluconate, detergent-based povidone-iodine or similar formulation. The process is similar to that described in **Figure 2**. The solution should be applied up to the elbow and vigorous washing should continue for a set period of time, in accordance with manufacturer's instructions, but typically for at least 2-3 minutes. The resultant lather should be rinsed off the hands/arms using purified hot water and ensuring the hands are kept higher than the elbows in order not to re-contaminate the hands. Taps should be turned off using the elbows or via foot pedal controls again to prevent re-contamination. Any excess water should be allowed to drip from the elbows as the hands/arms are dried thoroughly using sterile towels or hot air driers.

Gloving should be carried out in accordance with local procedures with frequent application of 70% v/v IPA. It is important to allow the alcohol to dry on the gloved hand before and during the gowning operation, to ensure good contact time with any microflora.

Regardless of how good the aseptic techniques employed within a cleanroom environment are, there should be frequent re-application of 70% v/v alcohol (e.g. isopropanol or ethanol-propanol blends) over the entire gloved hand, especially before carrying out critical activities within an EU GMP Grade A (ISO 14644 class 5) environment and after touching equipment. The frequent application of alcohol is important to prevent contamination transferring from one object to another and being distributed around the manufacturing area.

The alcohol should be applied carefully to one gloved hand and then spread gently and evenly over the other glove by carefully rolling the hands together to ensure completed coverage. Pre-sterilised alcohol sprays or alcohol streams are readily commercially available and afford a cost effective alternative to in-house preparation.

It is important to note that only a pure sterile mixture of 70% alcohol with 30% water for injection (WFI) should be used within this type of environment. Other preparations containing antiseptic additives should be avoided to prevent potential residue build up on hands and equipment.

2.7 International standards

European Standards EN 1499 and EN1500 (or equivalent international standards) specifies a method of test simulating practical conditions for establishing whether a hand sanitising agent for use on skin or gloved hands, reduces the release of transient flora, according to the requirements when rubbed onto artificially contaminated hands of volunteers (8,10). Standard EN 1499: 2013 refers to hand wash solutions and standard EN 1500: 2013 to handrubs. Obviously there are limitations to the methods employed in practice, especially when individuals in normal working environments do not employ the same hand-washing techniques and other factors such as skin disorders may hinder performance.

The EN 1500 method is more applicable to pharmaceuticals and healthcare. With this, the method involves applying live test organisms such as *Escherichia coli* to the hands, then recovering the test organism in order to obtain a baseline count. The test or reference disinfectant product is then applied to the hands before once again recovering any surviving test organisms in sampling broth containing neutralisers to terminate the effect of any residual agent. The organisms are enumerated and the difference between the numbers recovered from the test or reference, and baseline counts is established and statistically analysed for significance. The larger the difference between the two counts, the more effective the product. Each of the volunteers repeats the procedure for the reference and test product.

For the test product to conform to the standard, EN1500:1997, the mean log reduction should not be significantly smaller (at 90% significance level) than that obtained when using the reference product.

Certainly this type of test is a key indication of the effectiveness of any sanitising agents and a user should check that the formulation used does meet this standard as a minimum.

2.8 Training

Training plays a fundamental part in any contamination control exercise. The correct washing technique, type of sanitisation or antiseptic agent to be used, frequency of hand sanitisation and more importantly the consequences of not following the basic principles are key in ensuring the safety of patients, customers and ourselves.

Training sessions should be able to explain the basic principles and clear up any misunderstandings, they should highlight the risks with not performing hand sanitisation and start to introduce some of the products available.

Training kits are a useful addition to any practical training exercise. Individuals are encouraged to sanitise their hands using a special formulation which becomes visible under UV light. In this way the unwary volunteers can assess the right and wrong way to apply sanitising agents and frequently missed areas on the hand become easy to distinguish (refer to Figure 1).

Re-enforcement following a training exercise is key, so visible pictorial signs and guidelines next to sinks and sanitisation points on the ward or manufacturing environment act as a constant reminder to individuals of the importance of hand washing/sanitisation.

2.9 Summary

Hand washing is a critical activity to minimize the potential of cross contamination and preventing the spread of disease. The basic act of washing our hands is fundamental in protecting us and others from harmful pathogens, which are common in the environment we live in. Whether we use soap and water or specially formulated preparations it requires every person to correctly follow basic hygiene practice and help defeat the invisible enemy on our hands.

2.10 References

1. Kampf, G. and Kramer, A. Clin Microbiol Rev. Epidemiologic Background of Hand Hygiene and Evaluation of the Most Important Agents for Scrubs and Rubs 2004 October; 17(4): 863–893
2. Lowbury, E. J. L., Lilly, H.A., and Bull, J.P. 1963. Disinfection of hands: removal of resident bacteria. Brit. Med. J. 1:1251-1256
3. Talaro, K., and A. Talaro. 1996. Chapt. 13. Microbe-human interactions: Infection and Disease. Foundations in Microbiology: 387-389. W. C. Brown. Dubuque, IA.
4. Nobel, W. C. 1980. Carriage of microorganisms on skin. In Problems in the Control of Hospital Infection. S. W. B. Newsom and A. D. S. Caldwell, eds. Royal Society of Medicine. International Congress and Symposium. Series No. 23. Academic Press. London, UK
5. Nobel, W. C. and Pitcher, D. G. 1978. Microbial ecology of the human skin. Adv. Microbial. Ecol. 2:245-289.
6. Euradlex. The Rules Governing Medicinal Products in the European Community, Annex 1, published by the European Commission, 2009.
7. Beaney, A.M. (2005).Quality Assurance of Aseptic Preparation Services, 4th Edition, Pharmaceutical Press: London, UK.
8. Ayliffé GAJ, Lowbury EJC, Geddes, AM and Williams, JD (1992) Control of Hospital Infection: A practical handbook, 3rd Edition p.1. Chapman and Hall, London.

9. Tanzer JM, Slee AM, Kamay BA (1977) *Antimicrob. Agents Chemother.* **12** (6): 721–9. The mode of action of chlorhexidine. J Periodontal Res Suppl. 1973;12:68–75.
10. Anonymous: European Standard EN 1500. Chemical disinfectants and antiseptics, Hygienic handrub Test method and requirements), European Committee for Standardization: Brussels, 1997a.
11. Larson, E., Girard, R., Pessoa-Silva, C., Boyce, J., Donaldson, L. and Pittet, D. (2006). Skin reactions related to hand hygiene and selection of hand hygiene products, American Journal of Infection Control, Vol. 34, Issue 10, pp627-635
12. Huang, Y., Oie, S., Kamiya, A.: Comparative effectiveness of hand-cleansing agents for removing methicillin- resistant Staphylococcus aureus from experimentally contaminated fingertips. Am. J. Infect. Control 22, 224 ± 227 (1994).

CHAPTER 3:

SELECTION OF CLEANING MATERIALS

By Jasdeep Singh

3.1 Introduction

With all the advancements in cleanroom design one weakness lies in keeping surfaces clean, particularly when part of their function requires the transfer of materials and use by operators which are both potential sources of contamination. Careful consideration needs to be given to the routine removal of contamination. Complex air handling systems are quite efficient at removing airborne biological and particulate contaminants but if these contaminants adhere to surfaces then the ability of the HVAC (Heating, Ventilation and Air Conditioning) unit is limited.

Many measures have been taken to reduce the introduction of contamination and this occurs with a great deal of variance from one cleanroom to the next. It is imperative that the design of cleaning processes maintain the integrity of the cleanroom so it is fit for purpose and eliminates cross-contamination.

This chapter will focus on cleaning and disinfection materials and not sanitisation and sterilisation of materials, although there is a great deal of common ground between these processes. This chapter does not examine the cleaning of specialised manufacturing equipment and vessels as it outside the remit of this handbook.

Factors to be considered when designing a cleaning regime are

- Size of the unit
- Grade of room
- Surface materials
- Equipment for cleaning
- Throughput of materials
- Operator traffic
- Nature of the final product
- Ergonomics and ease of cleaning

These processes will require suitable materials to facilitate this process.

Regulators e.g. MHRA (1) and FDA (2) have set various limits of permissible contamination for each grade of room and subsequently operations in that room. There are even differences between various regulators on those limits in and out of use. If inadequate cleaning is carried out then these limits are frequently exceeded. A normal course of events when these limits are exceeded is to repeat a clean or have a more thorough cleaning process carried out, hence the critical nature of these procedures.

In order for the cleaning processes not to be the root cause for such excursions the choice and specifications of materials is critical. Inappropriate choices can either provide a further source of contamination or inadequate removal of any contamination due to operator difficulties or poor selection of equipment and materials.

There are a multitude of companies producing ranges of cleaning materials, tools and specialised equipment. The general principles are the same but there are some finer details which need to be addressed when choosing appropriate products. Costs play an important part in this exercise but the greater costs of failure should these products prove inadequate for your particular needs, should also be considered. Downtime will always be very costly due to lost productivity but products released with poor contamination control will destroy reputations very quickly. The relationship with your supplier is paramount to obtaining the correct and robust solutions for your needs.

This chapter will address some of these issues and also touch on some of the finer points which are sometimes missed, leading to disastrous consequences.

3.1 Wiping Materials

The basis of all cleaning requires a wiping agent or removal media. This could consist of the standard hand wipe right through to mop heads. The main purpose of the wipe is to facilitate the physical removal of any contamination and the distribution of cleaning agents to aid the chemical removal of contamination. Wipes can also become a source of contamination as they hold the contamination but do not necessarily lock in these contaminants. The frequency of use of material and any handling steps must limit the potential to redistribute any contaminants.

The choice of materials making up the wipe is a critical consideration. Materials that can become electrostatically charged in use as well as introducing electrostatic contamination to operating surfaces also then attract more charged particles. The attraction effect is quite desirable for picking up particles but does mean that surfaces susceptible to static build up become charged in the process. Synthetic materials are more likely to cause this.

Cleaning will precede disinfection and so the same wipes may be used in different ways to achieve this goal. The purpose of cleaning is to remove any surface contamination and changing the wiping material will lead to a reduction in cross contamination from wiping. This has to be done frequently enough, but if wipes, mop head and the like are changed too frequently this will add to costs and the time taken to carry out the cleaning tasks. A balance must be struck as to how often to change the wiping materials and how effective they are in operation in different areas. The lower the grade (e.g. EU GMP Grade C, D and unclassified) of room a more frequent approach to changing may be adopted as there is likely to be a greater load of surface contamination. This may be compensated for by the use of chemical agents which break down the contaminants. The use of chemical agents does have disadvantages that will be discussed later. If there is a heavier load of contamination an automated system may be used such as a vacuum cleaner to lower the load initially. A combination of equipment and processes may need to be used to serially reduce the contaminant load so as to improve the efficiency of the cleaning process.

Cleaning materials being used in the higher grade environments (EU GMP Grade A and B/ISO 14644 classes 5 and 7, in operation) should be sterile.

3.1.1 Hand wipes

Hand wipes come in many shapes, sizes, materials, dry and wet (pre-saturated). Each is designed to meet specific needs of the end user. This variety should meet the demands for a large scale pharmaceutical unit right through to the small scale hospital manufacturing units. Common principles apply to all areas but there are some specific requirements that are dependent on the different processes.

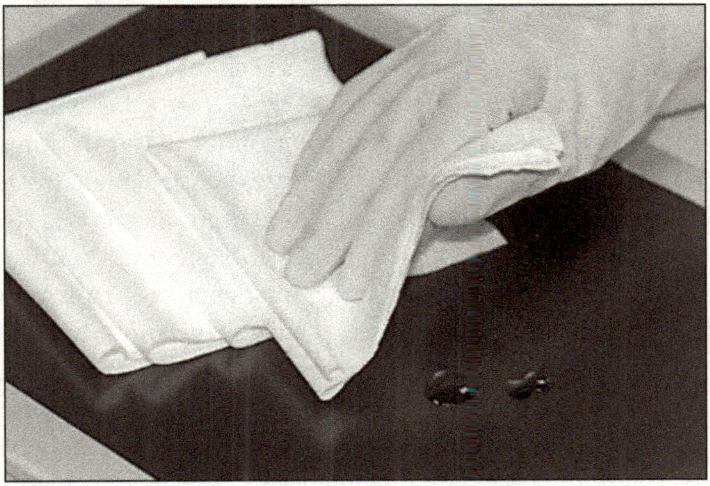

Figure 1 Multilayer wipe in use

Materials used in the manufacture of wipes vary to some degree but on the whole are a mix of polyester and cellulose. There are materials which are non-woven to reduce the potential for shedding particles and reduce the breakdown of the material matrix in use which could lead to further particle generation. These wipes can be described as lint free. Some wipes have laser sealed edges to reduce any particle generation and these should be used in all critical process areas where the potential to directly contaminate the product is high.

The polycellulosic wipes can also be multilayer wipes that are thermally bonded leading to greater absorbency properties and greater resistance to abrasion in use. These may also be laser edge sealed to reduce fraying at the edges and any particle generation. These are the main type of wipes likely to be used in the critical areas.

Cotton wipes are also available as either pure cotton wipes or a mixture with cellulose. These are woven in a tight twill construction reducing the chance of individual fibres splitting and breaking free from the weave. Otherwise this woven construction of natural fibres would have a tendency to shed fibres (lint). The material is further bleached, flame treated and mercerised to remove impurities which is a problem with natural fibres. This wipe has great absorbency properties together with a low static charge and nonabrasive characteristics but may be marginally more likely to shed fibres compared to the multilayer bonded wipe because of the nature of the fibre weave. In addition there may be trace impurities which may interact with cleaning agents leading to their deactivation.

A high absorbency foam hand wipe is also available that is made from polyurethane. The foam construction produces many air pockets that as well as holding onto liquid also hold onto contaminants. The characteristics of foam will allow the release of the liquids when pressure is applied so this is usually used to mop up liquids.

3.1.2 Impregnated wipes

Many of the previously mentioned wipes come impregnated or pre-saturated with cleaning agents. These wipes have always been considered advantageous over the use of dry wipes which then have to be impregnated either by being sprayed or soaked in a container. Spraying creates a lot a vapour causing lost agent to the environment and does not ensure adequate saturation of the wipe. Soaking the wipe may lead to cross contamination of the wipe depending on how frequently the reservoir is changed.

Examples of this include packs containing rolls of wipes (Figure 2) which are separated by perforations and contain liquid agents within the pack. Once these packs are opened the agent will evaporate over time and the benefit of impregnation lost. An additional problem for this pack is that the perforations do shed some particles when torn. These packs are suitable for unclassified or low grade areas for a first stage clean before entering assembly areas. These packs are usually not sterilised and when they are first opened will be exposed to the outside environment. These would not be suitable for use in critical process areas where sterile or aseptic manufacturing is occurring, but would be suitable for use in unclassified areas and low grade cleanroom areas.

Figure 2 Impregnated wipes on a roll

Alternative pack designs have smaller packs sealed in a plastic envelope that have a small peel away section that is usually re-sealable. These contain individual wipes that are pulled out of the pack without the need for tearing along the perforations. This reduces the chance of evaporation during the useable shelf life of the product from opening. In addition the chance of causing cross contamination of subsequent wipes removed from the pack is greatly reduced.

Impregnated wipes usually come in clearly labelled packaging which is critical as the choice of cleaning agent is quite specific and poorly distinguished packaging labelling could lead to operator errors.

The material must be inert to the agent for the shelf life of the product. Hypochlorites are known to react with polycellulose wipes over time so the chemical agent would be less effective over time. Another type of pack comes with the ability to impregnate the wipe at the time of use. This is a double pouch container with a breakable seal between the two compartments. One compartment will contain the wipes and the other a liquid cleaning agent.

3.1.3 Size of the wipe, pack sizes and pack presentation

Wipes come in a variety of sizes and are available as single packs and multiple packs depending on the user's requirements. The size of the wipe has to be considered depending on the activity that needs to be carried out. Operators will usually fold wipes so they are just larger than hand size. Operators would then refold wipes so that a fresh surface is exposed to the surface to be cleaned. This would otherwise be an effective method of cross-contamination if re-use of a heavily soiled wipe occurred. Operators need to be guided as to how often to refold the wipe, for example some units will refold the wipe after each single movement. This may be suitable for the particular environment particularly if the level of surface contamination is high or the surface area being cleaned is relatively small.

The number of wipes in a pack being used in critical areas is very important so that wipes are not wasted and are not stored in critical areas between sessions. Most manufacturers will have a selection of pack sizes. Individually wrapped wipes have advantages as they are less likely to be cross contaminated so there is very little wastage. The disadvantage however is when using multiple wipes per cleaning session in one area then you are introducing excessive amounts of packaging materials to that environment. Packaging material can produce particles and also harbour other particles. An assessment should be carried out as to the number of wipes to be used in a single session and pack sizes developed from there. There may be a need to be a range of pack sizes to meet the various needs for various operations in the different parts of the site; dry wipes can come in multiples of 100's in a pack which are suitable for large areas that are going to be cleaned in a session.

These large multipacks are much more cost effective per wipe but only if they are used up. Some units have risk assessed the use of these packs in lower grade areas where the pack may last a number of days. If there is a risk of contamination of the wipes in storage once the pack is opened, then this could be acceptable in certain circumstances. If this assessment was carried out in higher grade critical areas then there is a risk that the wipes may have a chance of contamination with prolonged exposure, which would not be acceptable for the specification required for these high grade rooms. This would lead to greater wastage and so it may be cost effective to use smaller packs. If costs are prohibitive then a time limit should be set for when multipacks are opened in the critical areas and the wipes should be disposed of or used in less critical areas after this time limit has been reached.

It would also be a prudent costing exercise to compare the cost of using impregnated wipes over dry wipes. Taking into account the time taken by operators to saturate wipes and the wasted liquid agents, it may be better to purchase a number of impregnated wipes but have a nominal number of dry wipes to give flexibility to use alternative agents.

As with any raw materials being passed into a number of areas until they reach critical processing areas, packs would benefit from multiple bagging. Double bagged systems are easier to sanitise into areas and so it would be beneficial to have packs bagged. Some consider triple bagging to be superior to double but the key point to consider is that the final bag is removed when being passed into critical areas. All the steps before that require removal of the outer bag and sanitisation of the remainder of the pack, but the same outer wrapping could be sanitised multiple times before entry to the critical zones. This should be risk assessed as to the necessity of double bagging over triple bagging as again the removal of each bag contributes to particle generation and additional waste being held in the unit.

3.2 Sterilisation of packs

Packs can be sterilised or not depending on where they are going to be used. Assessments should be made on whether the sterile wipe has an advantage in being used in low grade or unclassified areas where the benefits may be lost due to the level of environmental contamination. Various methods of sterilisation are used which will be discussed later, but individual packs should have an indicator on them to show that they have been successfully sterilised. Some companies put an indicator on the pallet packaging or on the secondary transportation packaging. Once the packs are removed from these containers, operators cannot identify them as being sterilised. Some companies provide a certificate of conformance on their packs. If this is the only pack available in the unit and the staff are trained appropriately then this is not a problem. If there is a choice then confusion can lead to the non-sterile packs being taken into the higher grade areas inappropriately.

3.3 Cleaning tool heads and mop heads

Domestic mop heads are designed for re-use and in the distant past this was deemed acceptable in some pharmaceutical areas. However these heads became a harbour for contaminants if they were not cleaned appropriately - a similar concept to the re-use of soiled hand wipes mentioned earlier. There are many common factors between the wipes and mop heads.

3.3.1 Material Properties

Mop head materials need to be sufficiently abrasive to remove contamination and be robust enough to deal with considerable surface areas and the need to transfer large quantities of cleaning agents to them quickly. Dry wipe heads can be as simple multilayer wipes that can be attached to an appropriate mop tool. They may have some light foam layer bound to them to allow for maintaining contact over uneven surfaces. Alternatives to this are microfiber heads that are electrostatically charged to attract and hold particles in during cleaning.

The greater part of mop heads for use with disinfectants are constructed using a polyester wipe bound to a much larger inner core of polyurethane foam. The foam gives the absorbance and the greater the amount of foam the larger the fluid capacity of the mop system. Some heads may just have the polyurethane foam but these are prone to damage and snagging when moved over uneven surfaces.

3.3.2 Shape and Size

Mop heads come in various shapes and sizes to meet an individual unit's needs. Large mop heads are suitable to cover large areas quickly but can be a problem when trying to access areas with restricted space. These mop heads are usually a rectangular shape to make good contact on large flat surfaces. Smaller size heads will take longer to cover the area by the operators but are likely to be able to cover dead spaces more easily.

Some heads are triangular in shape so as to access corners more easily. These types of heads are quite small and are normally designed for use in critical processing areas such as isolators. The heads are specifically made to fit a particular handle system and so you may find that you might need more than one manufacturer's system to meet all cleaning needs.

3.3.3 Single use systems

Mop heads are usually one off disposable use systems or ones that undergo a vigorous cleaning process to ensure cleanliness before the next use. They are normally designed for cleaning walls, ceilings and floors and usually require the use of a bucket.

A recent advance is a single use mop, head and bucket cleaning system which removes the need to ensure cleaning systems are clean before use.

Some companies will provide a service to clean and sterilise mop heads, but this is only viable if heads are removed once soiled and replaced. This would be suitable for high grade areas where the expected contamination load is low and hence the soiling rate of the wipe would also be low and so a single wipe would possibly suffice.

3.3.4 Tacky Rollers

An alternative to the dry wipe head is the tacky roller mop head. These are made up of polyethylene sheets which are used to pick up dust. As the sheets become soiled then they are peeled away to reveal a fresh sheet. These would only be used in low grade areas as an alternative to dry wipe cleaning prior to disinfection.

3.3.5 Specialised Tools

With these mop heads there are specialised tools to aid reaching and facilitate the operator's actions. The head should have a degree of rotation to be able to smoothly move across the flat surface without the operators tracking the movement of the head and having to apply any undue pressure as it moves further away. This could otherwise lead to a loss of surface contact as you try and reach the extremities. The shaft of the tool should be telescopic to stop operators from over reaching. This can be particularly problematical in isolators and laminar flow cabinets when you do not want the operator's upper body entering critical areas. The shape and size of the mop head has been discussed earlier, but the tool must be large enough to support the head and also have strong points of attachment so there is no free movement of the head during operations. The triangular shaped tool is specific for cleaning isolators and is designed for one hand use. It is light weight and the head only pivots in one direction giving better surface contact. The triangular tip is designed to be able to reach into confined spaces particularly corners.

The conventional mop handle and head frame normally would have pivoting abilities in two planes. This allows operators the flexibility to clean walls and ceilings without having to constantly readjust their body position. This system is made of an aluminium shaft and a PVC head to make it very light weight for the operators. The shaft can either be made up of a number of pieces or telescopic. This is extremely important when holding the mop above heads for prolonged periods as operators become fatigued they would lose contact with the ceiling surfaces.

Cleaning and sterilising telescopic shafts are more difficult as they have to be fully extended to clean and

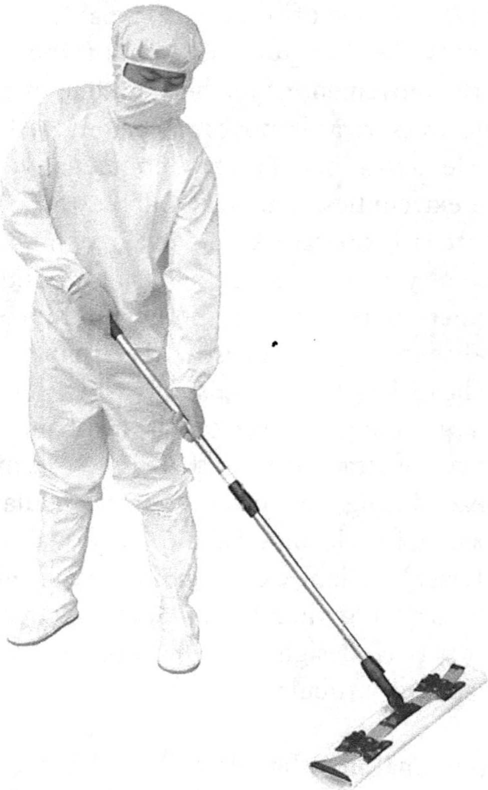

Figure 3 Conventional mop handle and head frame in use

sterilise properly. All these tools must be easy to clean and sterilise just as the cleaning heads associated with them.

3.3.6 Multiple bucket systems

Using a single bucket with the previously mentioned mopping tools, it would become very apparent that re-immersing the mop head into the bucket concentrates the contamination into a single reservoir. The mop head would become quickly soiled and not able to be cleaned during the mopping process. The only option would be to replace the mop head periodically. In order to preserve the integrity of the reservoir with the chemical agent it would be better to have a multiple bucket system with a ringer.

With a two bucket system the bucket next to the ringer contains water to rinse the mop head once soiled. The head should be rung through before being placed in the disinfectant containing bucket and then placed in the ringer before cleaning surfaces again. Excess solution would increase the drying time. A three bucket system involves rinsing in the middle bucket when the rear bucket is empty, so when the mop is rung the waste solution does not cross-contaminate the rinsing or disinfectant containing buckets (3). When rinsing the mop heads, care must be taken to ensure that the head does not touch the bottom of the bucket, as particulate contaminants settle at the bottom of the bucket.

3.4 Chemical Cleaning & Disinfection Agents

There is a very large choice of cleaning and disinfection agents available. Using single agents and combinations gives a broad spectrum of coverage. These products are also available in many different forms such as impregnated wipes mentioned earlier. Many companies produce a range of products to meet varying needs but there is no one ideal solution (4).

Ideal properties would be:

- Broad spectrum bactericidal, fungicidal, virucidal
- Active against spores
- Immediate action
- Penetrates organic matter
- Quick evaporation/ removal
- No residues
- Non-corrosive
- Chemically resistant
- Easily applied
- Safe for operators
- Inert breakdown products
- Ready prepared
- Not concentration dependant
- Deep penetration capability through any material
- Low retention time
- Low cost

With this extensive list of requirements it is not surprising that any one agent is unlikely to fulfil all these requirements. However, there is an ever increasing list of products that with combination agents will meet the majority of these requirements.

Table 1 summarises characteristics of commonly used agents. It should be noted that this table only has a few examples of each type of agent but new chemical derivatives are constantly being developed, each with improved characteristics. Single agent products of alcohol, surfactants, combinations of QAC's with biguanides or chlorinated based agents are common products. Some combination products may include some hydrogen peroxide. Much work has been done to optimise these products for normal use in cleanrooms and companies are keen to provide a vast array of supportive data. The cleaning agents selected should give good coverage of organisms including spores.

It should also be noted that agents can break down surfaces and can affect the seals of your units. Special care should be taken to remove any hypochlorite residues on metals due to its corrosive nature.

The effectiveness of an agent is dependent on:

- Type and quantity of the organism as this presents the specific level of challenge to the agent(s) and to the concentrations required
- Amount of protein based materials present as this tends to inactivate and absorb the disinfectant
- Presence of other organic compounds and soaps (e.g. non-ionic surfactants) either in the solution or on the surfaces, as these interact with certain disinfectants, even neutralizing them. In certain combinations this could enhance the effect for example quaternary ammonium compounds.

These factors must be considered when designing routine disinfection regimes. The solution will also be affected by other inherent characteristics namely pH, temperature, concentration and possible interactions between other agents and containers.

These solutions are available as impregnated wipes, ready to use spray bottles, large canisters and small

Disinfectant Category	Alcohols	Aldehydes	Biguanides	Chlorinating agents	Oxidizing Agents	Quaternary Ammonium Compounds (QAC)
Example	Denatured Ethanol Isopropyl alcohol	Formaldehyde Glutaraldehyde	Chlorhexidine	Bleach, Hypochlorite, Chlorine Dioxide	Hydrogen peroxide Peracetic acid	Diethyl ammonium chloride
Mechanism of Action	• Precipitates proteins • Denatures lipids	• Denatures proteins • Alkylates nucleic acids	• Alters membrane permeability	• Denatures proteins	• Denature proteins and lipids	• Denatures proteins • Binds phospholipids of cell membrane
Advantages	• Fast acting • Leaves no residue • Non-staining	• Broad spectrum	• Broad spectrum	• Broad spectrum • Short contact time, fast acting • Inexpensive	• Broad spectrum •fast acting •peroxide breaks down to water and oxygen	• Stable in storage • Non-irritating to skin • Effective at high temperatures and high pH (9-10)
Disadvantages	• Rapid evaporation • Flammable • hardens rubber • degrades glues	• Carcinogenic •Mucous membranes and tissue irritation • Only use in well ventilated areas •toxic •pungent order	• Active in pH range (5–7) •Stains	• Inactivated by sunlight • Requires frequent application • Corrodes metals •Mucous membrane and tissue irritation • Dilution reduces shelf life	• Damaging to some metals • Mucous membranes and tissue irritation •limited to surface activity due to poor penetration	•Narrow microbiocidal activity •Removes floor polishes
Vegetative Bacteria	✓	✓	✓	✓	✓	✓ —Gm Positive Limited—Gram Negative
Mycobacteria	✓	✓	Variable	✓	✓	Variable
Enveloped Viruses	✓	✓	Limited	✓	✓	Variable
Non-enveloped Viruses	Variable	✓	Limited	✓	✓	×
Spores	×	Effective	×	Variable	Variable	×
Fungi	Effective	Effective	Limited	Effective	Variable	Variable
Efficacy with Organic Matter	Reduced	Reduced	Reduced	Rapidly reduced	Variable	×

Table 1 Characteristics of Disinfecting Agents (5, 6)

bottles of ready to dilute concentrates. Products are available in non-sterile and sterile variations to allow for different working environments.

Companies have provided enough variations to meet individual needs but there has to be an appreciation of operator variance.

Some of these products leave residues which need to be cleaned with alcohols so doubling the cleaning process time. Alcohols should be used between detergents and biocides. If there is a retention time for the disinfectant then this must be adhered to before cleaning with alcohol. Operators must understand the differences between the products and the consequences of incorrect use.

3.4.1 Concentrates

The advantages of using concentrates over ready prepared solutions include ease of storage and the ability to vary the concentration according to needs. There is however a problem of the concentrates being quite corrosive and if not dissolved evenly can lead to ineffective cleaning.

3.4.2 Agent Rotation

There is an expectation that pharmaceutical manufacturers will rotate between two different agents on a routine basis (4). EU GMP states that more than one type of agent needs to be used but the aspect of rotation has crept in on the basis of keeping resistant organisms at bay. This means that if a resistant organism arises then a stronger third agent is brought in. The development of resistant organisms to disinfectants is a point of debate as this has been born out of resistant organisms to antibiotics, but not yet evident with disinfectants.

Some users have opted for the use of alcohol for cleaning and disinfection with a daily clean combination product. Here there would be careful trending data to observe the emergence of resistant organism and then a more specific disinfection product selected.

3.4.3 Container Design of Chemical Cleaning Agents

Due to the ever increasing demands of pharmaceutical manufacturers, much development has taken place with the disinfecting solutions presentation. One point of note is the standard 500-1000ml spray bottle. Originally the spray head was designed with a variable spray setting. This led to operators who would have the jet setting not giving even coverage over the surfaces and the solution effectively "bouncing off" the walls and ceilings. The opposite was true of too fine a spray setting. This led to the droplets not aggregating leading to dead spaces between the droplets; once the wipe was passed over this the droplets were absorbed and solutions did not cover the surface effectively. This led to spray heads being developed with on and off settings so the optimal droplet size range was produced even with the variance of pressure applied on the trigger spray.

There was then improved labelling of the bottles with greater distinctions between products to help avoid mistakes being made by operators. Some companies changed the label design giving increased prominence to the active agents and others introduced colour coded labelling.

A recent issue with the spray bottle has been the ingress of contamination into the reservoir of the bottle during use, due to suck back. One solution to the problem has been to introduce a collapsible bag inside the bottle which stops any vacuum being created and drawing back potentially contaminated air to prevent it from coming into contact with the solution (Figure 4).

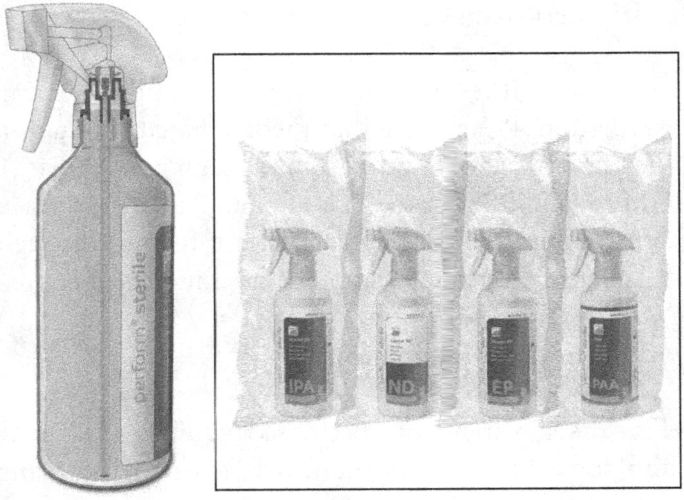

Figure 4 Collapsible reservoir system within a spray bottle.

3.4.4 Aerosols

Another spray device is the aerosol designed to make it easier for operators than pumping a trigger spray. These are initially very good as they give a fixed aerosol size but as the propellant concentration drops, the performance of the spray also does, sometimes leaving a large proportion of solution in the container.

Containers should have some tamper evidence to stop any contamination in use as they are sealed containers whose integrity needs to be maintained. It has been known for operators to open a spray bottle to quickly saturate wipe, then close the bottle and then use it to spray the walls of cabinets.

3.4.5 Sterilisation

Solutions either undergo filtration and or gamma irradiation. Please note that the irradiated products are the ones that should be used in the high grade areas (EU GMP A and B/ISO 14644 class 5 and 7 in operation) and even though the other solutions are filtered through a 0.2micron filter these should be used in the other areas.

3.5 Specialised Equipment

There is a variety of specialised equipment available and some in development which will aid the manual process of cleaning. Cleanroom vacuum cleaners were mentioned earlier particularly for use when there is a large degree of contaminants such as after a spillage. Wiping may lead to the contaminant being dispersed into the environment and hence enclosing the spill in the cleaner would be the best option. This HEPA (High Efficiency Particulate Air) filter cleaner must be regularly serviced and emptied.

Steam Cleaners are very good at cleaning and have some disinfecting properties but they leave water puddles as they cool and need to be mopped up. They are particularly good at removing organic material and do not leave any residues.

Vaporised Hydrogen Peroxide (VHP) cleaning systems have been developed for use in hospitals and other cleanrooms such as theatres. They really are for disinfection and can only disinfect exposed surfaces, but are sporicidal. VHP has a developing role in infection control management but the principle can be applied to pharmaceutical cleanrooms.

An ultraviolet (UV) light validation torch is a new product that will help to visually assess the effectiveness of cleaning and could become a great training tool.

3.6 Operator Issues

Using the best tools and equipment still does not overcome all operator issues. It is imperative that appropriate training and validation of the cleaning processes are carried out together with robust and rigorous environmental monitoring to keep cleaning issues in check.

3.7 Conclusion

There are many factors to consider when choosing materials to carry out the cleaning process but there are also many solutions available. Something as basic as a hand wipe, can offer a whole host of options, but choice should be seen as a good thing. There is no single magic system that will answer all the material selection problems, but a combination of systems will provide very effective systems. Material selection is just one part of the solution. Either systematic or on-going validation is essential in proving that seemingly inconsequential changes to cleaning systems do not affect the quality of the cleaning.

Research to improve materials is ongoing, but there is still a requirement for organisations to use their professional judgement to find the optimum balance between costs, operator ease and cleaning effectiveness together with the ability to prove the quality of cleaning instantly. All these materials together with robust regimens and systems will improve the quality of cleaning and reduce the chance of cleaning failure.

3.8 References

1. Euradlex. The Rules Governing Medicinal Products in the European Community, Annex 1, published by the European Commission, Brussels, Belgium, 2015
2. FDA. U.S. Pharmacopeia's Revised General Chapter <797> Pharmaceutical Compounding—Sterile Preparations: USP, Bethesda, MD, USA, 2013
3. Sandle, T. (2010) Cleaning Cleanrooms. *Cleanroom Technology*, 18 (12): 22-24
4. Sandle, T. 'Selection and use of cleaning and disinfection agents in pharmaceutical manufacturing' in Hanlon, G. and Sandle, T. (2015): *Industrial Pharmaceutical Microbiology Standards and Controls*, Euromed Communications, England, pp9.1-9.32
5. Gorman, S.P. and Gimore, B.F. Chemical Disinfectants. In Denyer S.P., Hodges N. & Gorman S.P.. Hugo and Russell's Pharmaceutical Microbiology 8th edition: Blackwell: London, 2011, pp312-333
6. Sandle, T. (2010) Choosing Disinfectants. *Cleanroom Technology*, 18 (9): 11-13
7. Tucker J., Simpson N. and Moss S. (2011) Trigger Happy: *Cleanroom Technology*, Vol. 19 at: http://www.cleanroomtechnology.com technical/article_page/Trigger_happy/60726

CHAPTER 4:

CLEANING TECHNIQUES

By Angela Nutman

4.1 Introduction

The effective cleaning and disinfection of a pharmaceutical cleanroom depends upon many factors. Consideration needs to be given to the choice of detergents and disinfectants used. However, the need for a robust procedure with effective cleaning techniques is also critical to the end result.

A written sanitisation programme is a regulatory requirement (1). It should specify all cleaning, disinfection and rinsing stages as well as the frequencies of each process and the techniques to be employed. The frequency of cleaning of each type of surface within each classification of room should be appropriate to the class of cleanroom and extent of its use.

Detailed written standard operating procedures (SOPs) should exist for each cleaning process and the specific techniques to be employed. Ongoing environmental monitoring must be performed in order to demonstrate the effectiveness of these techniques (1). Particular care should be taken to ensure the chosen agents are prepared, stored and used correctly within validated shelf lives and that equipment is used safely and effectively.

Staff training must be thorough and include competency assessment and periodic reassessment of technique in order to eliminate inter- staff variation in results achieved.

In this chapter the cleaning and disinfection stages required will be discussed, including the techniques considered to be best practice. The equipment available and how it may be used will be summarised, and staff training will be discussed.

4.2 Cleaning and disinfection stages of a sanitisation programme

The overall aim of a sanitisation programme is to reduce viable and non-viable contamination in the cleanroom to within the specified limits. EU GMP Annex 1 gives contamination levels for surfaces in different categories of cleanroom (1). Both cleaning and disinfection are required in order to achieve Good Manufacturing Practice (GMP) cleanroom standards of cleanliness but they should be considered as two separate activities. It is important that each is carried out at an appropriate time and frequency using validated procedures. Details of all stages should be specified in the programme including when cleaning alone is acceptable, when disinfection should be added, and when a more thorough clean should be undertaken, such as following commissioning or major works.

4.2.1 Cleaning

Cleaning is important for the physical removal of dirt such as dust, grease, skin particles, residue from cleaning agents and contamination from pharmaceutical raw materials or products (2). Prevention of cross contamination is especially important in hospital pharmacy cleanrooms which are often used for multiple product types.

Cleaning of surfaces is usually performed by application of neutral detergent with gentle agitation. See Figure 1 below.

If cleaning is performed effectively it should remove both viable and non-viable particles from the cleanroom and should be demonstrated by the environmental monitoring results. Regular cleaning may be all that is required if a cleanroom is consistently shown to be within the limits (3).

4.2.2 Disinfection

Disinfection is the destruction of viable organisms. The aim is to reduce the viable contamination to within a pre-defined limit. This accepted level of viable contamination is specified very clearly within the guidelines for pharmaceutical manufacturers (1).

Disinfection as an integral part of a sanitisation programme gives added assurance. It is usually performed by application of an appropriate biocide by either mopping, wiping or spraying. The biocide must be applied uniformly to the surface in the correct 'dosage' and be left in contact for the validated 'contact time' to be assured of being effective. For the biocide to take effect it needs to have direct contact with the surface. Therefore the surface must be free from dirt which could prevent direct contact with the surface and hamper the disinfection process.

Biocides with various modes of action exist. Appropriate agents should be chosen for the sanitisation programme and demonstrated to be effective by routine environmental monitoring. Alternating biocides with differing modes of action should be incorporated into the programme. This is a specific EU GMP requirement; the rationale for this is to avoid the emergence of microbial resistance to a single agent. If the monitoring shows a bacterial spore problem developing it is advisable to add a sporicidal biocide to the programme until the issue is resolved (3).

Care should be taken to avoid choosing unnecessarily harsh biocides for routine use. Some biocides are corrosive if left in contact with certain materials (especially stainless steel). It is possible for different agents to interact with each other. See Chapter 8 for further discussion of this.

Detergents and biocides will potentially leave unwanted residues on surfaces if not removed effectively. These residues may damage surfaces, provide a breeding ground for certain bacteria or build up over time and hamper cleaning and disinfection. It is therefore important that all agents are used in accordance with manufacturers' instructions and removed effectively following use.

Some biocides are designed to leave low levels of residue but still require a monthly or quarterly rinse to avoid build up. For surfaces where a pharmaceutical product is prepared it is best practice to wipe the area with sterile 70% alcohol or water of suitable quality (such as Water for Injections) to ensure complete removal (3). Alcohol impregnated wipes may be used to remove corrosive biocide residues from stainless steel surfaces. Prevention of biocide residue build up on walls and floors is best done by intermittent use of neutral detergent. Manufacturer of agents may also provide advice on a suitable procedure for residue removal.

4.3 Preparation of biocide or detergent solutions

For cleaning and disinfection to be an effective reliable process all detergent and biocide solutions must be prepared according to validated SOPs. If preparation errors occur then the product may be ineffective or harmful to staff or surfaces.

There are many cleaning and disinfection agents available in various presentations. See Chapters 5, 6 and 8. Solutions are typically supplied as ready-to-use solutions or as concentrates requiring dilution before use. Ready to use solutions may be the most simple to use but will require more storage space than concentrates. They may be impractical if large areas are to be cleaned.

Concentrates are designed to be diluted with water of a suitable grade for the cleanroom environment just before use. The water should be at room temperature only, unless validation has been performed at other temperatures. Manufacturers' instructions should be followed for dilution factors. If errors occur, the process could be ineffective if the resulting solution is too dilute. If the solution is too concentrated it may pose a hazard to staff or be damaging to the cleanroom surfaces.

It is important that solutions are only used within validated shelf life after preparation. It is good practice to label the prepared solution and use it immediately. Shelf lives of prepared solutions must not exceed the manufacturer's recommendation but should also be locally validated.

Only sterile agents must be used in GMP Grade A and B (ISO 14644 class 5 and 7 in operation) environments. If non sterile agents are used in GMP grade C and D environments they should be monitored for microbiological contamination (3). Many biocides are designed for single use only, rather than being stored. Some concentrates however are supplied in containers fitted with devices that have been validated to ensure that the contents remain sterile in use for much longer. A technical report detailing the manufacturer's validation work should be obtained and further local validation work performed to back up a decision to store solutions.

Concentrates supplied in suitable unit doses for preparation of the appropriate amount of solution are very practical, as this avoids the need to perform calculations and measure volumes of concentrates – both steps have the potential for error. This also has the merit of avoiding storage of concentrate once the container has been opened. Impregnated wipes avoid the need for dilutions and therefore reduce risk from an inappropriately prepared solution being used.

4.4 Application of detergent or biocide agent to cleanroom surfaces

When applying a cleaning or disinfection agent to a surface it is important to ensure even application to the whole of the surface, whilst avoiding spreading any contamination present. Cleanrooms ought to be designed without nooks and crannies where dirt might accumulate or cleaning might be difficult. It is also important to select suitable equipment and to employ techniques which are appropriate to the scale and design of the surfaces. It may be appropriate to use hand held impregnated wipes for cleaning and disinfecting equipment or bench tops, whereas ceilings, walls and floors will require either a mop and bucket system or a mop and impregnated wipe system.

The 'pull and lift' technique where the operator applies the agent with overlapping unidirectional strokes is often employed. See Figure 1. Each stroke is applied towards the operator (*pull*) and the wipe or mop is then lifted (*lift*). The next stroke is applied in the same direction overlapping the previous stroke by approximately 10%. This is repeated until the whole surface is covered. This technique ensures the whole surface is evenly covered and avoids spreading dirt around the surface. If gentle agitation is required to dislodge dirt stuck to a surface, the stroke is modified to involve backward and forward movement only within the stroke.

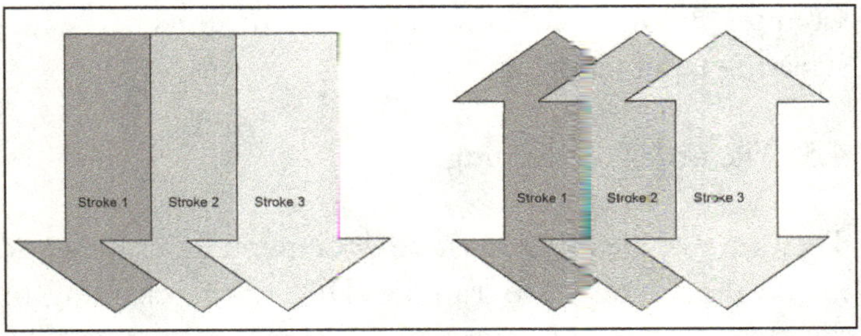

A. Without agitation B. With agitation

Figure 1. Pull and lift technique

When using hand held impregnated wipes the same pull and lift technique may be employed. Care should be taken to use any surface of a wipe once only. In practice a wipe is usually folded into a suitable size for use. After each stroke the wipe is refolded to expose clean fabric. The detergent or disinfectant should be sprayed onto the surface rather than the wipe and left for the required contact time before wiping is undertaken.

If using a mop and bucket, care must be taken to rinse and reload the mop frequently. Otherwise, dirt picked up by the mop will be moved around the surface and redistributed rather than being removed.

To remove residue from the surfaces a final stage in cleaning and disinfection is typically a rinse with a suitable grade of water. The same pull and lift technique will ensure residue is removed rather than just moved around the surface.

To aid such techniques commercial bucket and trolley systems are available. It is important to ensure only equipment designed for use in cleanrooms is used. See Chapter 3 for discussion of factors to consider when selecting equipment.

4.5 The order of cleaning

The order of cleaning must be documented in SOPs and in the sanitisation programme. During the cleaning or disinfecting process, care must be taken to avoid re-depositing dirt picked up from one surface onto another surface. The following points are best practice and should be incorporated into the cleaning SOPs.

1. Clean the cleanest areas first. For example, cleaning should commence from the room of the highest grade towards the unclassified environment (3). See Figure 2.
2. Start the process at a point furthest from the exit. If not, the operator will need to walk over cleaned floors to exit the room.
3. Start with high surfaces and work down. For example, clean ceilings before walls and walls before floors. This will prevent dirty cleaning solution dripping onto already cleaned surfaces.
4. Clean walls with a downwards overlapping stroke and avoid touching the floor with the mop.

4.6 Frequency of cleaning

The sanitisation programme should specify how often each room and each type of surface is cleaned. In general,

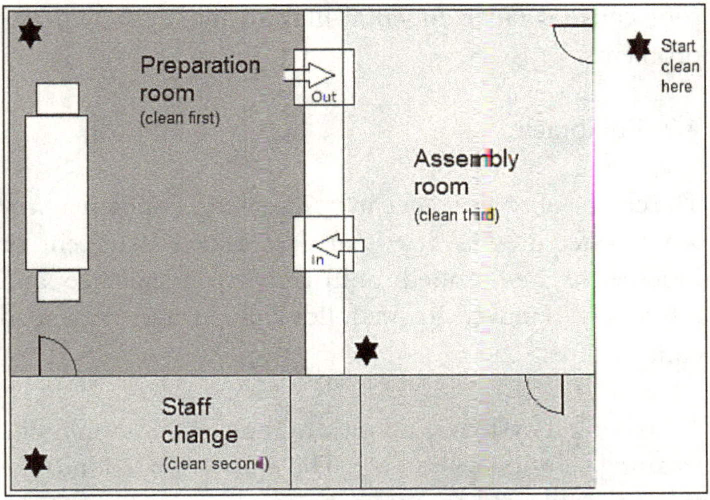

Figure 2. Order of cleaning or disinfecting a cleanroom suite

the higher the grade of cleanroom and the busier the cleanroom, the more frequent cleaning and disinfection will be required. Horizontal surfaces will require more frequent cleaning than vertical surfaces. Pharmaceutical product preparation areas require more frequent cleaning than support areas.

A typical regime might be quarterly cleaning of ceilings, monthly cleaning of walls, weekly cleaning of floors, and daily or sessional cleaning of benches. This would need to be supported by environmental monitoring results including contact plates of all surfaces.

A log should be kept of all cleaning and disinfection carried out, stating which agent was used and who performed the task. This will aid investigation into the root cause if environmental monitoring shows up any problems.

4.7 Equipment

The choice of equipment can be daunting. Fundamentally what is required is a system that allows detergent or biocide to be applied uniformly to a surface and effectively removed again following the recommended contact time.

The simplest system is a mop and bucket containing the cleaning solution to be used. The mop is dipped into the solution and used to apply the solution to the surface. The mop is dipped repeatedly into the solution leading to contamination of the solution and poor efficiency. This system may be acceptable in a domestic setting but is not appropriate when trying to achieve a GMP standard of cleanliness.

An improvement on this is a 'double bucket system'. This consists of a bucket containing the cleaning solution and a second bucket containing clean water with a wringer above. See Figure 3. The mop is dipped into the cleaning solution and used to apply it to the surface. Before dipping into the solution again, the mop is rinsed in the clean water and wrung out. Any dirt picked up by the mop will end up in water rather than in the cleaning solution. The water will become contaminated leading to lower efficiency when rinsing the mop.

A further improvement is the so called 'triple bucket system'. In this system the wringer is above a third bucket. This is empty initially and will collect waste. See Figure 4. After the mop has been used to apply solution to a surface, it is wrung out over the empty bucket, rinsed in the clean water and wrung out again. The mop may then be reloaded with cleaning solution. This system minimises the contamination of the clean water and cleaning solution therefore improving efficacy of the cleaning process.

Commercial systems are available that include buckets, wringers and mops transported on a trolley. Both double and triple bucket systems can be sourced. The design of mop varies according to classification of cleanroom and type of surface it is to be used for. See Chapter 3 for discussion of the important factors when designing a cleaning system.

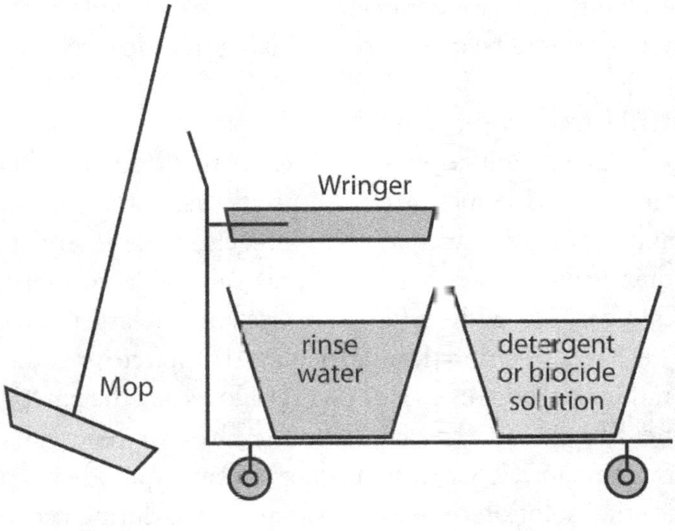

Figure 3. Double bucket system

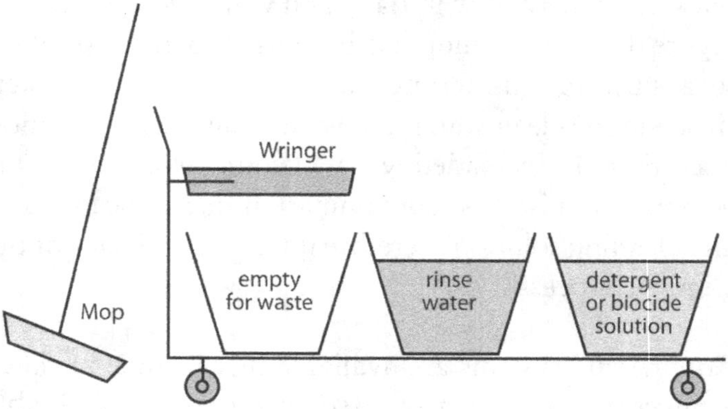

Figure 4. Triple bucket system

Storage of a triple bucket system will require more room than a double bucket system. However, it has been demonstrated that a triple bucket system improved the effectiveness of cleaning and disinfection of a cleanroom (4). It is therefore recommended that use of a triple bucket system should be considered in high grade cleanrooms.

Sterile mop wipes impregnated with various cleaning and disinfectant agents are also available. Hand held impregnated wipes are commonly used for transfer sanitisation of raw materials into cleanrooms and for equipment and benches, but are also available on a larger scale for use with a flat mop system on larger areas. They are available as low particulate or lint free for highest grade cleanroom use. Use of wipes allows an efficient 'pull and lift' action thereby ensuring physical removal of contaminants. There is no bucket system required, and no cleaning solution to become contaminated during use. As there is no dilution of concentrates to be performed, there is no risk of error of dosage. However, the flat mop head does require skill in order to ensure even application to the surface.

The level of saturation of a wipe is always consistent, ensuring controlled application of the fluid to the surfaces, providing the wipes are only used to cover a suitable area otherwise they may become dry and less efficient.

Dedicated equipment only should be used for the specified cleanrooms and should be stored appropriately to minimise contamination during storage (2). For example, cling film may be used to wrap equipment after it is cleaned and ready for use. Mop heads must be either disposed of after use or re-sterilised (2). See Chapter 2 for further discussion of equipment available.

4.8 Staff training

Cleaning and disinfection are critical stages in a pharmaceutical cleanroom. For them to be effective, the sanitisation programme must be adhered to, biocide and detergent solutions must be prepared and used correctly, equipment must be stored, assembled and used appropriately and any problems must be reported and dealt with effectively. For all of this to happen, the staff carrying out the cleaning and disinfection must have the appropriate training and understand why they are doing things in a particular way. Given the critical nature of the cleaning and disinfection processes, it may be prudent to use expert staff contracted from a specialist cleanroom disinfection service.

The training programme should cover the specific cleaning and disinfection procedures and the relevant health and safety aspects. It must also provide a background understanding of GMP. All training, assessments and reassessments of competence must be documented and records kept on file for each member of staff.

Staff may need to handle corrosive biocides or clean surfaces where contamination from hazardous medicines may be present. Therefore, appropriate personal protective equipment suited to the task must be supplied. Clothing must also be suitable for the cleanroom environment.

4.9 Summary

This chapter has described the importance of a written sanitisation programme specifying the key stages for the cleaning and disinfection of cleanrooms. Good practice techniques commonly employed and the equipment systems available have been discussed, along with the importance of thorough staff training.

For a sanitisation programme to be effective it must be designed specifically with the grade of cleanrooms and their intended uses in mind and be carried out by suitably competent staff. Routine environmental monitoring must be in place to demonstrate its effectiveness. There are key principles that should be borne in mind when designing the programme as follows:

1. Cleaning and disinfection are distinct processes. Both are required in GMP cleanrooms.

2. Appropriate choice of detergents and biocides must be made for the specific circumstances.
3. All agents must be used according to validated SOPs.
4. Residues must not be allowed to build up.
5. Start cleaning at the point in a room furthest from the exit and work towards the exit.
6. Clean the cleanest areas first. For example, clean higher grade rooms and critical areas before cleaning lower grade support rooms.
7. Clean high fixtures and surfaces first. For example, clean a ceiling and light fittings before cleaning a wall or floor.
8. Clean walls from top to bottom.
9. Clean floors last.
10. Wipe surfaces using a pull and lift technique (with or without agitation). See Figure 1.
11. Do not allow agents to be in contact with surfaces for longer than the manufacturer's recommended contact times.
12. Do not allow solutions to run into areas that may not be easily reached for residue removal.
13. Consider use of triple bucket systems or impregnated wipes to improve the efficacy of cleaning and disinfection processes.
14. Horizontal surfaces will require more frequent attention than vertical surfaces.
15. Higher grades of room and high traffic areas will need more frequent attention.

4.10 References

1. Euradlex. (2015). The Rules Governing Medicinal Products in the European Community, Annex 1, published by the European Commission, Brussels
2. Beaney, A.M. (2005). 'Quality Assurance of Aseptic Preparation Services' 4th Edition, London: Pharmaceutical Press
3. NHS Pharmaceutical Quality Assurance Committee, (2008). 'Cleaning and Disinfection Regimes for Cleanrooms' 1st Edition, London: National Health Service
4. Smith, J. (1999). 'The effect of different cleaning methods on environmental monitoring' National QA Symposium, Grantham.

CHAPTER 5:

SAFE USE OF DETERGENTS AND DISINFECTANTS

By Ian M. Jarvis

5.1 Introduction

This chapter aims to give the reader a broad appreciation of the safe use of detergents and disinfectants in everyday settings within the healthcare and pharmaceutical environment. Unfortunately the terms, detergent and disinfectant cover a very broad range of chemicals used widely in the home, industry and healthcare settings, covering thousands of uses, from cleaning hospital wards to washing laundry. Added to this complexity is the variation in potential hazards associated with the use of these compounds.

Because of their common use there is a vast array of legislation controlling their use and disposal, with countries adopting different approaches over their application and control. Fortunately for the user the task of complying with local laws and regulations resides with the manufacturer, who is legally bound to ensure the user is supplied with enough information to ensure it is safe to use. This information may be as simple as a label or more comprehensive and supplied as a material safety data sheet.

5.2 Regulation of Disinfectants and Detergents.

5.2.1 Disinfectants

In Europe, the EU Biocides Regulation 528/2012 sets up a European Community product authorisation scheme for biocidal products (1), such as non-agricultural pesticides, disinfectants and preservatives. The Directive has the central objectives of harmonising the European market for biocidal products and their active substances, and providing a high level of protection for humans, animals and the environment. The regulation is implemented in each Member State according to their own legislative system. The scope of the regulation is very wide, and not only covers disinfectants but also pest control products and preservatives. It has three main aims:

- To harmonise the European market for biocidal active substances and products containing them.
- To provide a high level of protection for humans, animals and the environment.
- To ensure that products are sufficiently effective against target species.

There are three main criteria addressed: 'chemistry', 'efficacy' and 'human health'.

If a component of the disinfectant falls within this legislation then there are strict controls over how the product can be advertised, packaged and labelled and also the type of information that needs to be available to users and the responsibilities placed on manufacturers. In the U.S., disinfectants and biocides must be registered with the Environmental Protection Authority (EPA) and meet the Occupational Safety and Health Administration's requirements for Occupational Exposure to blood borne Pathogens (29 CFR 1910) as well proper management of any waste when disposed, which is regulated under the Resource Conservation and Recovery Act (RCRA). Similar registration programmes are in place in other parts of the world.

5.2.2 Detergents

In Europe, EC Regulation No 648/2012 covers any substance or preparation containing soaps and/or other surfactants intended for washing and cleaning processes. Detergents may be in any form (liquid, powder, paste, bar, cake etc.) and marketed for use in household, institutional or industrial purposes.

The objective of the Directive (2) is to establish rules designed to achieve the free movement of detergents and surfactants on the internal market while, at the same time, ensuring a high degree of protection of the environment and public health. It harmonises rules on the biodegradability of surfactants in detergents, imposes restrictions or bans on surfactants on grounds of biodegradability, makes provision for the additional labelling of detergents including fragrance allergens and the information that manufacturers must hold at the disposal of the Member States' competent authorities and medical personnel.

Related regulations for detergents include: Regulation (EU) No 259/2012, which imposes a restriction on phosphates in domestic laundry and dishwasher detergents; and Detergents Regulations 2010 SI740, which places some restrictions on inorganic detergents in certain settings.

In the U.S., detergents need to conform to the requirements of the Food and Drug Administration (FDA). The exception is with 'soap', which falls under the Consumer Product Safety Commission (CPSC).

5.3 Choosing the right detergent or disinfectant

Many factors need to be considered before choosing a detergent or disinfectant; these include the physical, chemical and toxic properties as well as working practices and area in which the substance is to be used.

It is always good practice to try and use the least toxic or weaker formulations first, if these prove fit for purpose then it makes no sense in exposing the worker or the surface on to which the substance is to be used to harsh chemicals.

In settings where resources are limited (3), it is important not to waste money on expensive cleaning products that are unnecessary. Where the volume of intended use is high, preparing cleaning solutions from bulk products should be considered. For smaller facilities, it may be necessary to purchase commercial products for use in cleaning high-risk areas, such as an operating theatre or clean room, to ensure that cleaning meets the requirements for the area. What is important is that the decision as to what product(s) to buy or use is not left to chance but through careful selection criteria.

Things to consider include:

- Will the chemical need to be diluted. If it does, what with and do you have the facility to do this safely?
- Is it safe to use on the skin or only on inanimate surfaces and do you need a high, medium or low level of disinfection/cleaning?
- What is the exposure/contact time?
- Does the detergent/disinfectant need to be washed off after use?
- Stability and expiry date of both the bulk concentrate and the dilution.
- Will it leave a residue on the surface?
- Is it easy to use?
- Any special storage conditions, flammable, corrosive etc?
- What personal protective equipment will be required, if any?
- Availability and customer service, what is the lead time for repeat orders?
- What are the disposal requirements/environmental impact?
- Cost effectiveness
- Bacterial resistance, will it be effective on different types of bacteria/moulds?
- Mode of application wiping, brushing, spraying or misting.

It should be noted that many of the chemical disinfectants/detergents are proprietary prepared formulations and their chemical components although listed on the label may not give full details of individual concentration.

Most cleaning products contain either non-ionic surfactants (emulsifiers and detergents), anionic surfactants or a mixture of both in their composition. In solution, non-ionic surfactants are electrically neutral, but anionic surfactants carry a negative charge within their structure. When detergent is applied to a soiled vertical surface the bulk of product runs off within a given time. However, a small but finite amount of detergent remains on the surface and contains some of the anionic surfactant which was present in solution originally applied to the surface. If the surface is not thoroughly rinsed prior to the application of a quaternary disinfectant, the disinfectant can be totally inactivated. In solution, quaternary salts, such as benzalkonium chloride are positively charged and can therefore combine readily with the negatively charged anionic residue and become totally inactivated. For these reasons it is important to fully understand what the disinfection/cleaning process is trying to achieve and have some basic knowledge of the formulations to be able to make an informed decision.

5.4 Safety in use

Chemical disinfectants and /or detergents could be hazardous to individuals if they are not properly handled, some of the chemical disinfectants are flammable, potentially explosive and some can react with incompatible chemicals violently and generate toxic gases (5). All chemical disinfectants are, by their very nature, potentially harmful or toxic to living organisms. Like other toxic substances, they could be harmful to humans upon entering the body; however, chemical disinfectants are an effective and safe tool when handled properly with adequate safety measures in place.

Most disinfectants and detergents can cause irritation to eyes, skin and/or the respiratory tract, therefore, the safety of all personnel should be considered. Training on proper storage, mixing and application procedures is essential (4). Personal protective equipment (PPE), such as gloves, masks and eye protection should be worn during the mixing or application of disinfectants. All chemical disinfectants should have a Safety Data Sheet (SDS) or a Material Safety Data Sheets (MSDS) (terminology varies worldwide). These sheets list the stability, hazards and personal protection needed, as well as first aid information. This information should be available to all personnel.

As general principles the following areas need to be considered when working with detergents and disinfectants:

- Be sure you can read all labels and follow the instructions for use, do not be tempted to "add a bit more" to the dilution or over dilute.
- Use protective clothing/equipment provided.
- Do not mix chemicals.
- Never put chemicals into unmarked containers.
- Never put chemicals into bottles or containers which had previous uses i.e. fizzy drink bottles.
- Be sure to know the first aid treatment required if you accidentally spill or ingest the chemicals.
- Store the chemicals correctly.
- Report any faulty equipment, spillage or damage to containers.
- Always follow the standard ways of working and develop safe working practices.

5.4.1 Labelling

A plethora of potentially confusing information is included on the label of any bottle of disinfectant or detergent. None of it is particularly relevant unless it can be interpreted (7,8,9). Legislation does differ from country to country, but as a minimum the following labelling aspects should be covered:

The labels must contain:

- The name of the manufacturer.
- Weight or measures in the container.
- List of active and inactive ingredients. The active ingredients of the product are listed as percentages and are the chemicals responsible for the control of the micro-organisms. Inactive ingredients are often lumped into one statement and include items such as soaps or detergents, dyes or colouring agents, perfumes, and water.
- List of warnings and first aid instructions.
- Measures to be taken if the product is swallowed or spilled on the skin/clothing.
- Registration No. with the relevant environmental protection agency or equivalent agency.
- Directions for use:
  - Dilution ratio
  - How to apply
  - Whether rinsing is necessary or not
  - How long to be left on surface
  - Where not to use

The Precautionary Statement describes the potential hazards of the product (to people or animals) and actions to take to reduce those hazards (i.e., wearing gloves or goggles). Specific "signal words" are used to indicate the degree of hazard. Descriptors used (from least harmful to most harmful) are: "Caution", "Warning", "Danger" and "Danger-Poison". A pictorial descriptor is also included on the label to act as a visual indicator of the risk associated with the use of the product (refer to Figure 1).

The "First Aid" section lists the actions to take in the event of accidental swallowing, inhalation or contact with the product. A "notes to physicians" area may be listed with specific medical information needed by medical professionals.

Additional Precautionary Statements contained on the label include extra safety and precautionary information such as environmental hazards, physical or chemical hazards, (i.e. corrosiveness or flammability), and storage and disposal information.

The "Directions for Use" section tells what the product controls, as well as where, how and when to use it. Some products may have multiple uses (i.e. cleaning versus disinfection), require different dilutions and/or contact times for such specific actions. The best application method to use with the product (i.e. spray directly or wipe on surfaces) will also be listed.

5.4.2 Hazard Warning Symbols

All over the world there are different laws on how to identify the hazardous properties of chemicals or chemical 'classification' and how information about these hazards is then passed to users, through labels, and safety data sheets.

This can be confusing because the same chemical can have different hazard descriptions in different countries. For example, a chemical could be labelled as 'toxic' in one country, but not in another.

The United Nations (UN) brought together experts from different countries to create the Globally Harmonized System of Classification and Labelling of Chemicals (GHS).

The aim of the GHS is to have, worldwide, the same:

- Criteria for classifying chemicals according to their health, environmental and physical hazards; and
- Hazard communication requirements for labelling and safety data sheets.

The UN GHS is not a formal treaty, but instead is a non-legally binding international agreement. Therefore countries must create local or national legislation to implement the GHS. **Figure 1,** gives some of the common traditional warning symbols found on disinfectants and detergents, while **Figure 2** lists some of the newer symbols which will be appearing in the future.

Toxic | Harmful/Irritant | Corrosive

Figure 1 – Traditional Hazard Warning Signs (some common examples)

Corrosive

Toxic

Dangerous to the environment

Caution - used for less serious health hazards like skin irritation

Figure 2. New International Hazard Warning Signs (some common examples)

5.4.3 Stability, Storage and Handling

Some disinfectants, such as bleach (sodium hypochlorite) lose stability quickly after being prepared for use or when stored over long periods, especially in the presence of heat or light. Disinfectant product labels will list the shelf life of the concentrated product, but often neglect to inform the user of the limited life following dilution. To maximize stability and shelf life, products should be stored in a dark, cool location and preferably in stock concentrations. Use of an outdated or inactivated product may result in the use of a non-efficacious product and will lead to a false sense of security (6).

General storage considerations should include the following:

- Store the detergent/disinfectant as per the manufacturers' instructions

- Keep out of the reach of children and pets.
- Don't transfer to other containers.
- Rotate stock using oldest first.
- All containers should be clearly and accurately marked with contents.
- Store rooms need to be well ventilated, especially if they contain large volumes of material.
- Adequate lighting to prevent inadvertently using the wrong material.
- A lockable door or secure area.
- Bulky and heavy items should be stored near the floor.
- Keep out of direct sunlight.
- Maintain a steady temperature.
- Keep containers tightly closed.
- Do not store with PPE to prevent cross contamination.
- Adopt best Manual Handling considerations when handling, carrying and dispensing.

5.5 Risk Assessments

To ensure the health and safety of employees engaged in handling disinfectants/detergents, a carefully planned chemical safety programme is essential. The aim of a chemical safety programme is to systematically identify and investigate potential hazards in order to minimize the risk of adverse health and safety effects due to exposure to chemicals in the workplace. In the programme, the chemical hazards of chemical(s) should be firstly identified. The risks arising from these hazards are assessed taking account of the work situations and personnel involved. Appropriate preventive and/or control measures are then set up to eliminate or mitigate the risks, with their effectiveness being regularly monitored and reviewed. The associated hazard information and protective measures should be communicated to all affected employees. The chemical safety programme should also include other elements like planning of emergency responses and training of employees.

Many factors can influence the risk of hazards associated with chemical disinfectants/detergents in the workplace. These include physical, chemical and toxic properties of the material, work practices, the nature and duration of the exposure, the effects of combined exposures, the routes of entry into the human body, and the susceptibility of the worker.

Reference should always be made to relevant local legislation, codes of practice, guidelines and best trade practices in order to decide on the need and adequacy of safety measures. Employers should keep an inventory of all chemical substances in the workplace, identify whether they are hazardous and ensure that they are handled and stored safely. It is also essential to obtain the Material Safety Data Sheet (MSDS) (or equivalent) of the chemical from the suppliers, as it contains a wealth of information indispensable for risk assessment, stipulation of safety measures and emergency planning.

An example of a formal risk assessment approach in the UK is found within The Control of Substances Hazardous to Health Regulations 2002 (COSHH). This is a legal framework to protect individuals against risks from hazardous substances used at work; hazardous substances are substances that may cause health problems including asthma and dermatitis. Other countries have very similar legislation in place, but generally all follow the same basic control steps and assessment process.

Under the COSHH Regulations, all activities which involve potential exposure of any person to a substance hazardous to health must be subject to an assessment. Control options must be defined such that risks to health are prevented or, where this is not reasonably practicable, adequately controlled.

COSHH sets out 8 basic measures that must be used as an approach when using hazardous substances in the workplace.

Step 1 - Identification of the Hazards and Assessment of the Risks

Identification of the hazardous substances present in the workplace and considerations of the risks these substances present to people's health.

Step 2 - Decide what Precautions are Needed

If significant risks are identified, deciding on the action to take to remove or reduce them to acceptable levels.

Step 3 - Prevent or Adequately Control Exposure

If it is reasonably practicable to do so. Things that might be considered include:-

- changing the process or activity so that the hazardous substance is not needed or generated;
- replace it with a safer alternative;
- use it in a safer form, e.g. pellets instead of powder.

Step 4 - Ensure that Control Measures are Used and Maintained

COSHH requires that controls, safeguarding against exposure to hazardous substances, are inspected and maintained. The objective being to ensure that every element of the control measure continues to perform as originally intended. This applies to items of equipment such as extract systems, personal protective equipment and to systems of work, which need to be regularly checked to make sure that they are still effective. COSHH set specific intervals between examinations for extract systems, and records of examinations and tests carried out (or summary of them) need to be maintained for at least five years.

Step 5 - Monitor Exposure

People performing the hazardous substance risk assessments (COSHH assessors) must consider whether there is a need to measure the concentration of hazardous substances in the air breathed in by individuals. It would be required where:

- There could be serious risks to health if control measures were to fail or deteriorate.
- Exposure limits could be exceeded.
- Control measures are not working properly.

Step 6 - Carry out Appropriate Health Surveillance

Individuals performing the hazardous substance risk assessments must consider if health surveillance is appropriate as part of the COSHH risk assessment.

Substances that may require health surveillance include:

- Substances of recognised systemic toxicity (it must be possible to detect the disease or health effect),
- Substances known to cause occupational asthma.
- Substances known to cause dermatitis.
- Certain specific substances under the appendices of the COSHH regulations.

Step 7 - Prepare Plans and Procedures to Deal with Accidents, Incidents and Emergencies

Where a work activity gives rise to a risk of an accident, incident or emergency involving exposure to a hazardous substance, which goes beyond the risk associated with normal day to day work, plans and procedures to deal with such events must be prepared.

Step 8 - Information, Instruction and Training

If you work with hazardous substances you should:-

- Be aware of the risks associated with them.
- Have access to a risk assessment.
- Know how to use personal protective equipment and clothing provided.
- Know how to ensure that any extract system you use is working properly.
- Be given the results of any exposure monitoring and health surveillance.
- Be given training in any emergency procedure, which you may need to follow.

5.6 Personal Protective Equipment

Protective clothing protects the skin or personal clothing from contact with chemical disinfectants/detergents and prevents spread of contamination. When handling these materials while dispensing or conducting work processes, individuals should always wear suitable protective clothing. Protective clothing can includes gloves, aprons, gowns and overalls and it is extremely important to choose protective clothing made of materials that resist penetration or damage by the chemicals involved (12,13,14).

Gloves are probably the most common form of personal protective equipment (PPE) used to protect individuals against damage to health from skin exposure. Exposure to harmful disinfectants and detergents can result in effects on the skin e.g. irritation, burns or allergic dermatitis, or in systemic effects after absorption or penetration through the skin. Generally household disinfectants and detergents are safe to use without wearing gloves, however even washing up liquid will eventually start to affect the normal oils present on the hands and could lead to mild dermatitis.

Key factors to assess when choosing a glove are:

- How the glove is to be used
- The length of time the gloves are to be worn
- The specific chemicals that will come in contact with the glove
- The environmental conditions, e.g. temperature of the solution

- Will the gloved hands be immersed in the liquid for long periods of time?
- Will the task lead to a puncture or abrade the glove?
- Will the glove prevent adequate dexterity?
- What the glove is made from
- Glove length
- Glove thickness
- Glove finishes and linings

5.7 Material Safety Data Sheets

Within Europe safety data sheets have been made an integral part of the system of Regulation (EC) No 1907/2006 (REACH) (11). A similar enforcement is in place in the U.S. and other territories.

Material Safety Data Sheets (MSDSs) are a widely used system for cataloguing information on chemicals, chemical compounds, and chemical mixtures. MSDS information may include instructions for the safe use and potential hazards associated with a particular material or product. These data sheets can be found anywhere where chemicals are being used. They are not primarily intended for use by the general public but more by the manufacturer in an occupational setting.

An MSDS provides an important source of information about a specific chemical used in the processing work, especially when the chemical is used for the first time. The information includes safe handling and storage of the chemical, first-aid procedures, potential effects of contact and measures to take in the event of a spill or leak. ISO 11014-1 (10) recommends a standard format for the MSDS, which contains the following sixteen sections or headings of information:

1. Product and company identification;
2. Composition/information on ingredients;
3. Hazards identification;
4. First-aid measures;
5. Fire-fighting measures;
6. Accidental release measures;
7. Handling and storage;
8. Exposure controls/personal protection;
9. Physical and chemical properties;
10. Stability and reactivity;
11. Toxicological information;
12. Ecological information;
13. Disposal considerations;
14. Transport information;
15. Regulatory information; and
16. Other information.

5.8 Disposal

Correct disposal of detergents and disinfectants will vary and there is no better advice than to read the label or material safety data sheet. Generally both detergents and disinfectants are safe to wash down the drain during normal use, i.e. for washing hands and cleaning floors, however they can cause a serious environmental impact if large quantities of undiluted bulk material enters the surface water drains.

It is often illegal, as well as unsafe, to dispose of hazardous materials improperly. Waste of different natures should be disposed of in separate containers labelled with the name and type of the chemical waste in a prominent area according to their chemical nature. Chemical waste should be held in containers of suitable design and construction to prevent leakage or spillage of the contents under normal conditions of handling, storage and transport.

As well as careless and illegal disposal, spillages can often lead to an inadvertent discharge of chemicals. In the event of spillage do not allow product to enter drains, prevent further spillage if safe to do so and use clean up using an absorbent material then transfer to suitable, labelled containers for disposal.

5.9 Summary

In our modern world detergents and disinfectants are indispensable and serve as effective and safe tools when handled properly with safety measures in place, however if misused, they can be hazardous and harmful to individuals and the environment.

Most countries have their own legal controls in place and although some harmonisation has taken place, there are still some differences in approach, therefore users must always refer to local legislation when dealing with chemicals, such as detergents and disinfectants.

Thankfully better labelling, safety information, secure packaging and better understanding of risk assessments have all helped in ensuring that individuals can feel confident in using these chemicals on a day to day basis.

5.10 References

1. EU Biocides Regulation 528/2012 (EU BPR), European Commission, Brussels, Belgium.
2. Regulation (EC) No 648/2012 of the European Parliament and of the Council of 31 March 2012 on detergents, which came into force on 8 October 2005.Articles 9 and 11 and Annex VII of Regulation 648/2004 impose numerous obligations on manufacturers to provide information about their products on labels and data sheets.
3. South East Asia Regional Office (SEARO), World Health Organization. 1988. *A Manual on Infection Control in Health Facilities*. SEARO: New Delhi, India, pp 72–88.
4. Ewart SL. Disinfectants and control of environmental contamination. In: Smith BL. editor. Large Animal Internal Medicine: diseases of horses cattle, sheep and goats. 3rd edition. 2001. St. Louis: Mosby. pp. 1371- 1380.
5. Centers for Disease Control and Prevention (CDC). 1991. Chlorine gas toxicity from mixture of bleach with other cleaning products. *MMWR* 40(36): 619–621.
6. Shulaw WP, Bowman GL. Disnfection in on-farm biosecurity procedures. The Ohio State University Extension Fact Sheet VME-8-2001.
7. Integral Asepsis Forum, Detergency and its role in Disinfection (Corlstadt, N.J.: *Airwick Industries, Inc.* (1975).
8. Lowbury, E.J.L., Geddes, A.M. and William, J.D. (1998): Control of Hospital Infection (A Practical Handbook); 3rd Edition: *Chapman & Hall Medical*, Landon Chapter 5 & 6.

9. Maurer, I.M. (1985): Hospital Hygiene; 3rd Edition, *Richard Clay (The Chaucer Pdren) Ltd.*, Great Britain.
10. Safety data sheet for chemical products, ISO 11014-1:2009, International Organization for Standardization, Geneva, Switzerland.
11. Regulation (EC) No 1907/2006 of the European Parliament and of the Council of 18 December 2006 concerning the Registration, Evaluation, Authorisation and Restriction of Chemicals (REACH), establishing a European Chemicals Agency, amending Directive 1999/45/EC and repealing Council Regulation (EEC) No 793/93 and Commission Regulation (EC) No 1488/94 as well as Council Directive 76/769/EEC and Commission Directives 91/155/EEC, 93/67/EEC, 93/105/EC and 2000/21/EC (OJ L 396, 30.12.2006, corrected version in OJ L136, 29.5.2007, p.3).
12. ASTM F 739-99a, Standard Test Method for Resistance of Protective Clothing Materials to Permeation by Liquids or Gases Under Conditions of Continuous Contact. This test method measures the resistance of protective clothing materials to permeation by liquid or gaseous chemicals under the condition of continuous contact.
13. Rawson BV, Cocker J, Evans PG, et al. (2005), Internal contamination of gloves: routes and consequences. Ann Occup Hyg 49:535–41
14. Labour Department, Chemical Safety in the Workplace – Guidance Notes on Personal Protective Equipment (PPE) for Use and Handling of Chemicals, 1st edition, 2002, HKSAR Government.

CHAPTER 6:

APPLICATION OF DISINFECTANTS AND DETERGENTS IN THE HEALTHCARE SETTING

By Eric Che

6.1 Introduction

Cleanliness in healthcare settings has been a key focus in recent years as it intrinsically links to healthcare associated infection (HCAI). Addressing HCAI requires a multidisciplinary approach together with full management support. The use of disinfectants and detergents is integral in the cleaning process and thus to contamination control.

In this chapter, the following topics will be covered: trend and measure of HCAI, microorganisms of interest contributing to HCAI, drivers for cleaning in the healthcare setting, disinfectant agents used in the environment and for device decontamination, and advanced decontamination methods.

6.2 Trend in Healthcare Associated Infection (HCAI) surveillance

HCAI is a generic term encompassing infections in any part of the body system, including the urinary tract infection (UTI); hospital acquired pneumonia (HAP), the skin, surgical site infection (SSI), gastrointestinal system and more severely, bacteraemia. These infection sites are displayed in Figure 1 below.

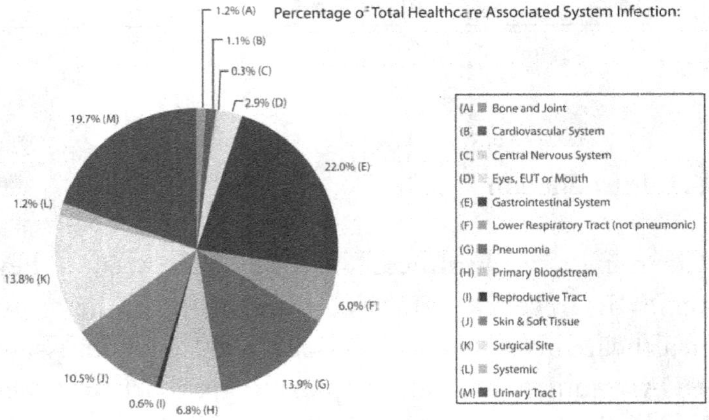

Figure 1: Summary of Results of the Prevalence Survey of Healthcare Associated Infections in Acute Hospitals, England, Hospital Infection Society and Infection Control Nurses Association, 2012

As an example, acute trusts in England have been reporting all *Staphylococcus aureus* (including methicillin-resistant *Staphylococcus aureus* – MRSA) bacteraemia on a voluntary basis to the Health Protection Agency (HPA) since 1990. These data show that during the 1990s MRSA bacteraemia increased dramatically - from fewer than 100 in 1990 to more than 5000 in 2001. Since 2014, improvements have been seen with levels at the 1000 mark. The proportion of all *S. aureus* bacteraemia that were methicillin-resistant also increased significantly - from fewer than 5 per cent in 1990 to more than 40 per cent in 2001 and to above 60 percent a decade later (1). Although part of the increase could be attributed to better identification techniques and improved reporting awareness, it was apparent that MRSA was becoming a significant problem in hospitals.

Surveillance or monitoring of HCAIs is fundamental to their control. Many hospitals in England have participated in voluntary surveillance of key infections for many years. However, as part of the increased focus on control of HCAIs, surveillance of some infections was made mandatory. *Staphylococcus aureus* MRSA bacteraemia reporting was made mandatory in April 2001. This was later extended to glycopeptides resistant enterococcal (GRE) bacteraemia in October 2003 and *Clostridium difficile* infection (CDI) in January 2004. The latest additions were: methicillin-sensitive *S aureus* (MSSA) bacteraemia in January 2011 and *Escherichia coli* bacteraemia in June 2011 (2).

In 2004, the UK Department of Health introduced a target to reduce MRSA bacteraemia across all National Health Service (NHS) acute hospitals and acute foundation trusts by 50 per cent by 2008. At the end of the first quarter 2008, the NHS had achieved a 57 per cent reduction in MRSA bacteraemia against the 50 per cent national target. The reduction in MRSA bacteraemia continued with a total of 1,481 cases of MRSA bacteraemia reported across the NHS between April 2010 and March 2011. This represents a reduction of 22 per cent on the total number of cases reported in the same period in 2009 and 2010, where 1,898 cases were reported and a 50 per cent reduction on the number of cases in the year before.

Thirty-five NHS organisations had been free from MRSA bacteraemia for 12 months in November 2011. This is more than double the fourteen organisations who achieved this in May 2010 and just four trusts were free from MRSA in September 2006 (3). This trend is shown in Figure 2 below.

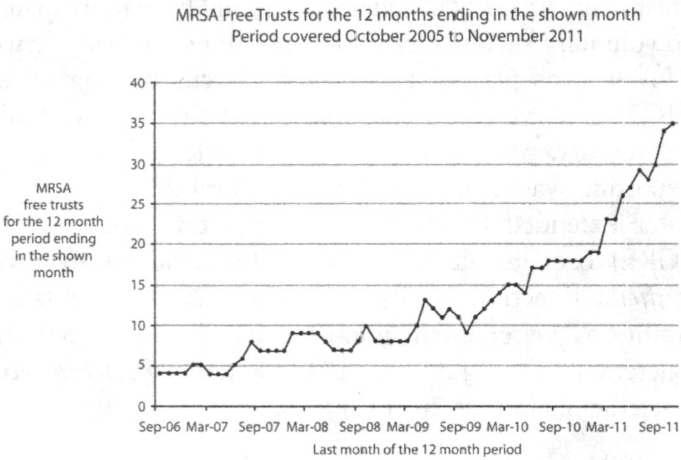

Figure 2: Trend in MRSA free NHS Trusts since 2006

Despite the progress made in reducing the incidence in MRSA bacteraemia, the UK government made it clear that the NHS should adopt a zero tolerance approach to all avoidable healthcare associated infections. Outlined in the NHS Operating Framework (4) and the associated Technical Guidance (5), new targets have been set to further reduce the incidence of HCAI. The targets are a further reduction for MRSA bacteraemia and 17% reduction for *C difficile* respectively. If these targets are achieved, the annual number of MRSA bacteraemia will be reduced down to below 1000 and reduce *C difficile* infections from to below 15,000. Similar targets have been set across European Union member states and in the U.S.

6.3 Microorganisms of interest

Methicillin resistant *Staphylococcus aureus* (MRSA)

MRSA are mainly transmitted by direct person-to-person contact, usually via the hands of healthcare workers and through environment contamination (6). The *MecA* gene is the essential determinant of methicillin resistance in MRSA. *MecA* is a 2130-bp segment of DNA coding for a penicillin-binding protein (PBP2' or PBP2a) characterised by a low affinity for most beta-lactams and which is thought to take over the functions of all other PBPs when they are saturated by methicillin or other beta-lactam antibiotics.

Molecular techniques for the detection of *MecA* are the gold standard for determining resistance. Polymerase chain reaction (PCR) for amplification of the staphylococcal *mecA* gene can be performed within a few hours. As an alternative, commercial kits are available. Disc diffusion and breakpoint methods are widely used. Other methods give more rapid results i.e. a latex agglutination-based method detects PBP2a protein and is commercially available.

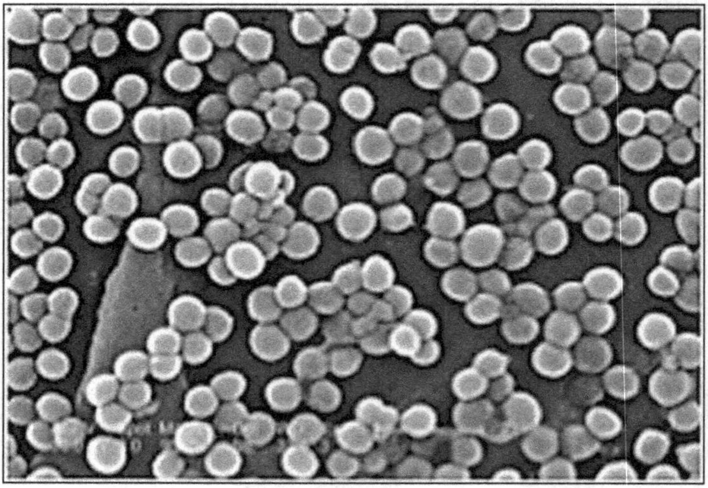

Figure 3: Scanning electron micrograph (SEM) depicted numerous clumps of methicillin-resistant *Staphylococcus aureus* bacteria [Centers for Disease Control and Prevention]

Clostridium difficile

C.difficile is a Gram-positive rod, spore forming and strictly anaerobic bacteria (7). The name "difficile" is a testament to the difficulties experienced in the early culture and characterisation of the species. Toxigenic strains produce large protein toxins A and B which are the major virulence factors. The production of toxins A (enterotoxin) and B (cytotoxin) causes the characteristic mucosal damage resulting in plaque-like lesions and formation of a pseudomembrane in the gastrointestinal tract leading to the characteristic symptoms. Not all strains of C. *difficile* produce toxin and therefore not all infections are symptomatic.

The presence of C *difficile* toxins in diarrhoeal stool is generally regarded as suggestive of CDI in the absence of any other recognised cause for gastrointestinal symptoms. Tissue culture for the detection of C. *difficile* toxins by its cytopathic effect (neutralisable with C *sordillii* antitoxin) requires technical expertise and requires up to 24-48 hours for the final result. There are numerous commercially available tests intended to detect the C *difficile* toxin. Some detect Toxin A, others A and B, although the sensitivity and specificity of these are variable. Tests that detect both toxins A and B are more appropriate than those which detect A alone, because not all strains produce toxin B without toxin A production.

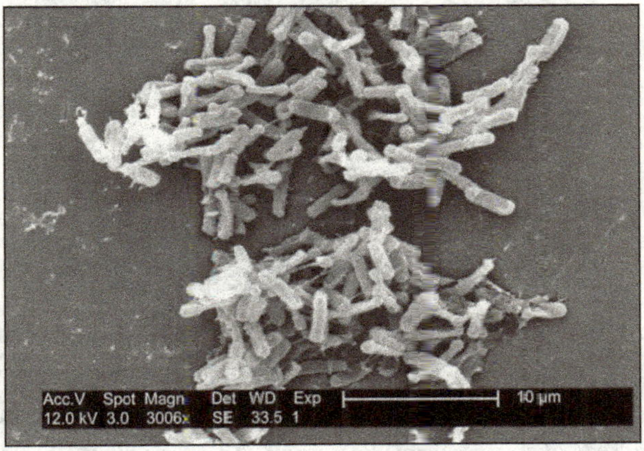

Figure 4: Micrograph depicts Gram positive C *difficile* bacteria from a stool sample culture obtained using a 0.1µm filter. [Centers for Disease Control and Prevention]

Escherichia coli

E. coli bacteria exist in many different types and strains. Non-virulent strains of *E coli* make up the major proportion of the natural flora in the gastrointestinal tract in humans and animals. Although harmless in the gastrointestinal tract, strains of *E coli* outside the normal habitat can cause serious infections. Potentially dangerous *E coli* can exist transiently and harmlessly on the skin surface, predominantly between the waist and knees.

There is an emerging trend of antibiotic resistance over the last 40 years, with particular significance to *E. coli*. This is largely due to the transmittance of resistance genes exchange between different *E coli* cells. NDM-1 is one of those genes responsible for resistance to carbapenems.

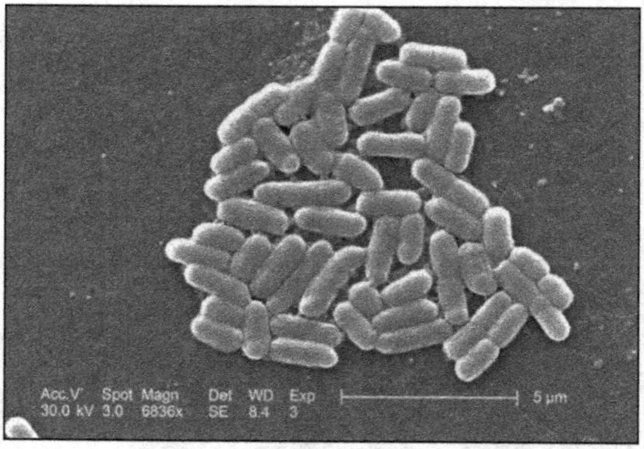

Figure 5: Under a magnification of 6836x, this colorized scanning electron micrograph (SEM) depicted a number of Gram-negative *Escherichia coli* bacteria of the strain O157:H7, which is one of hundreds of strains of this bacterium. Although most strains are harmless, and live in the intestines of healthy humans and animals, this strain produces a powerful toxin, which can cause severe illness. [Centers for Disease Control and Prevention]

6.4 Cleaning drivers in healthcare

This section examines some of the important guidelines relating to the cleanliness of healthcare facilities.

The Health and Social Care Act 2008 – Department of Health

Within the UK an important driver for healthcare cleanliness is set out in the Code of Practice on the prevention and control of infections under the Health and Social Care Act 2008 (8). The scope of the code of practice includes all registered providers of all healthcare and adult social care in England. Part 3 of the code of practice sets out the ten criteria against which the Care Quality Commission (CQC) will judge a registered provider on how it complies with the cleanliness and infection control requirement, which is set out in regulations.

Section 21 of the Healthcare and Social Act 2008 enables the Secretary of State for Health to issue a Code of Practice about healthcare associated infections. The Code contains statutory guidance about compliance with the registration requirement for cleanliness and infection control (regulation 12 of the Health and Social Care Act 2008 (Regulated Activities) Regulations 2010). The law states that the Code must be taken into account by the CQC when it makes decisions about registration against the cleanliness and infection control requirement. The regulations also say that providers must have regard to the Code when deciding how they will comply with registration requirements.

The CQC may use its enforcement powers or take other actions where it decides that a registered provider is not meeting its legal obligations as set out in the regulations. It will reach this decision by looking at whether a registered provider is doing what is set out in the Code. If a registered provider is not following the Code, then the CQC will want to consider whether that is because it is not appropriate to the type of service being provided. If it is appropriate, the CQC will want to consider whether a registered provider is still protecting people from the risk of infection in another equally effective way. The key criteria within the Act are summarised in the table below.

The Revised Healthcare Cleaning Manual 2009

Within the UK, the National Reporting and Learning Service (NRLS) has worked jointly with the Association of Healthcare Cleaning Professionals and NHS Purchasing and Supply Agency (PASA) on behalf of the National Patient Safety Agency (NPSA) (9). The resulting manual supersedes the previous NHS cleaning manual. The document outlines best practices of cleaning applicable across different healthcare provision environments, including acute care, mental health care, primary care and the ambulance service. There is also a collection of cleaning method statements and advice on the use of emerging cleaning techniques. This manual is a valuable reference to homogenise cleaning standards in the healthcare setting.

Table 1: "Code of Practice" for all providers of health care and adult social care on the prevention and control of infections under the Health and Social Care Act 2008.	
Compliance Criterion	**What the registered provider will need to demonstrate**
01	Systems to manage and monitor the prevention and control of infection. These systems uses risk assessments and consider how susceptible service users are and any risks that their environment and other users may pose to them.
02	Provide and maintain a clean and appropriate environment in managed premises that facilitates the prevention and control of infections.
03	Provide suitable accurate information on infections to any person concerned with providing further support or nursing/medical care in a timely fashion.
04	Provide suitable accurate information on infections to any person concerned with providing further support or nursing/medical care in a timely fashion.
05	Ensure that people who have or develop an infection are identified promptly and receive the appropriate treatment and care to reduce the risk of passing on the infection to other people.
06	Ensure that all staff and those employed to provide care in all settings are fully involved in the process of preventing and controlling infection.
07	Provide or secure adequate isolation facilities.
08	Secure adequate access to laboratory support as appropriate
09	Have and adhere to policies, designed for the individual's care and provider organisations that will help to prevent and control infections.
10	Ensure, so far as is reasonably practicable, that care workers are free of and are protected from exposure to infections that can be caught at work and that all staff are suitably educated in the prevention and control of infection associated with the provision of health and social care.

NPSA colour coding hospital cleaning materials and equipment

In relation to the UK, in 2007, NPSA launched a colour coding scheme for cleaning materials and equipment (10). It was designed to help hospitals reduce the risk of cross infection by segregating cleaning equipment used in different areas from the clinical areas. For example: red for bathrooms and yellow for isolation rooms. This is to ensure materials and equipment are not used in multiple areas. The ultimate aim is to improve the safety of hospital cleaning, ensure consistency and provide clarity for staff.

Deep cleaning initiative

A further UK venture was the national deep cleaning initiative which was launched by the Department of Health in 2007 (11). Several deep cleaning activities were suggested in the deep cleaning programme; however, flexibility was built in to enable local decision on the actual deep cleaning measures. Benefits achieved with the initiative included raising the profile of cleaning and prioritising the funding available to cleaning. The deep clean initiative is not a one-off exercise and NHS trusts are expected to ensure that deep cleaning is an important component in their cleaning arrangements. Deep cleans can be used in addition to routine periodic cleaning routines and as a remedial action in cases where deficiency of routine cleaning is identified.

Figure 6: Colour coding hospital cleaning materials and equipment

6.5 Cleaning agents in hospital

The choice of cleaning and disinfection agents used within a hospital is an important one. An ideal disinfectant should have the following properties (12):

- Broad spectrum of activity: viricidal, bactericidal, sporicidal.

- Have no issue with development of resistance.
- Non-corrosive.
- Non-hazardous.
- Easy to use.
- Minimal contact time.
- Active on a wide range of surfaces.
- Active in presence of organic matter.
- Economical to use.
- Easy to store and distribute.

Unfortunately the perfect disinfectant is yet to be invented. Therefore there is a range of disinfectants and detergents in use in hospitals. Some of these different disinfectants are discussed next with consideration given to the mode of actions and advantages and limitations to match a particular application

Alcohol containing products:

The mode of disinfection action of alcohol is the denaturation of proteins. Alcohols are effective against many bacteria including *Mycobacterium spp*. and fungi. They have variable activity against viruses and have no activity against bacterial spores. Alcohol does not penetrate well into organic matter, particularly proteinaceous material and should only be used on physically clean surfaces. In the healthcare setting, alcohol containing products are a mixture of water soluble alcohol i.e. ethyl alcohol and isopropyl alcohol.

Example presentations:

- Industrial methylated spirit (IMS) 70%

- Alcohol swab (small swab so add in 70% isopropyl alcohol) e.g. "Mediswab"
- Alcohol wipe (large wipe soaked in 70% isopropyl alcohol) e.g. "Alcowipe"

Chlorhexidine products:

Chlorhexidine is easily inactivated by soap, blood or other organic material and should only be used for skin disinfection. It should not be used directly on brain tissue, meninges or perforated ear drum.

Example presentations:

- Scrub solutions: Chlorhexidine gluconate 4% in detergent solution (Hibiscrub), Chlorhexidine gluconate 0.5% in 70& isopropyl alcohol with emollient (Hydrex/Hibisol).
- Skin Preparations: Chlorhexidine in spirit (0.5% chlorhexidine gluconate in 70% IMS);
- Chlorhexidine gluconate 2% in 70% isopropyl alcohol – line insertion and care; chlorhexidine in spirit with red dye – to colour skin.
- Wound cleansers: Aqueous chlorhexidine 0.05% in 25mL sterilised sachets (Unisept)
- Bladder irrigation: Aqueous chlorhexidine acetate 0.02% (Urotainer Chlorhexidine)
- Instrument disinfection: Chlorhexidine in spirit with 0.1% sodium nitrate as rust inhibitor.

Detergents

Detergents are useful in the removal of organic material from equipment. They function to loosen grease and dust.

Example presentations:

- General purpose detergent: Hospec

Chlorine containing products:

The active ingredient is chlorine which has a broad spectrum of antimicrobial activity including viruses. Chlorine based products are the disinfectants of choice during a "clinical" clean involving spillage of blood or other body fluid.

Example presentations:

- Sodium hypochlorite solution 1% (Milton and granules (Haztabs)

Superoxidised water

This is used in endoscopy. Superoxidised water is produced by a microprocessor sterilisation system on site. The cold sterilisation solution is non-toxic and non-hazardous to staff.

Cleaning regime and frequency

A daily clean with a detergent product is adequate in most clinical areas. In these areas, there is a need to remove organic matter and dust together with bacterial load in the environment. The domestic staff should have received training and all areas are subjected to regular audit on the standard of cleaning. An additional deep clean is available on the advice of the infection control team. For example in cases of an infection outbreak, a chlorine based agent should be used on all hard surfaces and uncarpeted floors. There is also a specific procedure on dealing with blood spillages. Isolation rooms or areas where service users have a transmissible infection are recommended to be cleaned daily using a chlorine based product.

A terminal deep clean will be required at the end of the isolation period and prior to the admission of a new patient. All bed linen will need to be disposed of as specified by the laundry requirements. Soiled or infectious laundry should be placed in an alginate bag and then in a red linen bag for cleaning. The segregation of infectious laundry from socially soiled laundry prior to washing is important. Curtains should also be laundered.

Hydrogen peroxide vapour (HPV) gassing technology is increasingly popular in the healthcare setting. Decontamination using HPV technology is applicable in both outbreaks of infection as well as in decontaminating newly built or refurbished clinical areas where there is a high bioburden in the environment. The technology provides a log 6 reduction of bioburden in the area and there is evidence supporting its efficacy.

Decontamination of medical devices

The Microbiology Advisory Committee to the Department of Health (MAC Manual), Sterilisation, Disinfection, and Cleaning of Medical Equipment:

Guidance on Decontamination, classifies the risk of infection associated with the decontamination of medical devices as (13):

(a) **High risk** - In close contact with a break in the skin or mucous membrane or introduced into sterile body areas. Equipment used in this situation should be sterilised when re-processed e.g. surgical instruments, endoscopes and implants.

(b) **Intermediate risk** - In contact with mucous membranes; contaminated with particularly virulent or readily transmissible organisms; or prior to use on immunocompromised patients. Equipment used in this situation requires disinfection or sterilisation e.g. respiratory/anaesthetic equipment, bedpans.

(c) **Low risk** - In contact with healthy skin or not in contact with the patient. Equipment used where there is no contact with the patient should be cleaned. But if the equipment is in contact with healthy skin, cleaning may not be sufficient in some cases e.g. trolley tops, operation tables, baths.

Decontamination of endoscopes

Both rigid and flexible scopes are decontaminated using a validated endoscopic reprocessing system which complies with the national standard. The UK Medicines Healthcare products Regulatory Agency (MHRA) has identified that agents contaminating an endoscope can originate from failures in the decontamination process, from contamination during storage, or from previous patients (14).

It is recommended that equipment is single use where possible. Channel cleaning brushes and, if a biopsy has been taken, the valve on the biopsy/instrument channel port used with flexible endoscopes should be disposed of as clinical waste after each use. Single use, disposable biopsy forceps should be used routinely in all patients to prevent the risk of seeding. Seeding refers to the transfer of malignant cells to the subsequent user of the endoscope.

The MHRA suggests that decontamination should begin as soon as possible after endoscopes and their accessories have been used. This should begin with thorough manual cleaning using a suitable detergent and suitable cleaning brushes, in accordance with the endoscope manufacturer's instructions. This will involve dismantling the endoscope and cleaning it carefully with brushes, paying particular attention to long narrow lumens and occluded surfaces. Then there should be a thorough rinsing. The use of ultrasonic baths and enzyme detergent solutions for cleaning endoscope accessories is also recommended where the process is compatible with the device.

For bronchoscopes specifically, after removal from the patient, and before washing, the scopes should undergo leak testing. A designated leak-testing device should be connected to the bronchoscope, air turned on and then the bronchoscope immersed in clean water with no detergent. If a leak is detected, visible by a continuous stream of bubbles, the scope should be wiped clean and sent for repair. After manual cleaning of the scopes, the instruments must be either disinfected or sterilised. For flexible scopes this can be achieved by using an automated endoscope reprocessor (AER). It is essential that the AER machine has itself been properly cleaned and disinfected before use, employing where possible the AER's self-disinfection cycle to include all fluid pathways, tanks and immersion trays.

The microbiological quality of the rinse water and other fluids must be acceptable because there have been reports of procedure acquired infection from contaminated rinse water. Final rinse waters are sent weekly for a total viable count (TVC) and for mycobacteria quarterly as per the requirement of Health Technical Memorandum 2030 (15) and Working Party Report, 2002 (16).

The final stage of the process is drying and ensuring safe storage. Rigid scopes should be stored in the packaging in which they were sterilised. Flexible endoscopes should generally be stored suspended vertically in ventilated storage cabinets, to allow the circulation of air. They should not be in contact with other endoscopes or flat surfaces.

Precautions for preventing vCJD transmission

There are additional precautions for the decontamination of flexible endoscopes used in all patients with definite, probable or possible Creutzfeldt-Jakob disease (CJD), and in those identified as at risk of developing CJD. In these cases, the decontamination needs to be sufficiently robust to ensure that any prions are inactivated. The use of non-fixative disinfectants is preferable if compatible with the manufacturer's instructions. Disinfectants with fixative properties should not be used in this case as these will stabilise prion.

6.6 Advanced Decontamination Methods

Ultraviolet light germicidal irradiation (UVGI)

UV radiation inactivates microorganisms by absorption of the UV light, causing a photochemical reaction that disturbs molecular components critical to cell survival. When the UV light penetrates the cell of the organism, the energy of the UV light reacts with nucleic acids and other cell components. The end result is cell injury or death. The UV spectrum is divided into UV-A (400nm to 315nm), UV-B (315nm to 280nm) and UV-C (280nm to 200nm). Although the entire UV spectrum is active against microorganisms, 265nm is the optimum wavelength. Most UV lamps provide UV-C energy at a wavelength of 254nm by electrical discharge through low pressure gas enclosed in a quartz tube. The two principal UV disinfection modes are: low pressure lamps producing maximum energy output at 253.7nm or medium pressure lamps producing energy from 180nm to 1370nm. Alternatively, other wavelengths can be used at a high intensity in a pulse manner.

The survival of a microbial population exposed to UV light is an exponential function of the UV dose. In general, bacteria are more susceptible to UV disinfection than fungi; viruses and spores are moderately susceptible to UV light exposure.

UV light in the application of disinfection is an established method in water systems. Hospital room disinfection using UVGI can be achieved by continuously disinfecting the upper air of the room with appropriate shielding of the occupants. Alternatively, the UVGI component can be installed within the HVAC system and disinfect the air circulation passing the UVGI unit. More recently, the application of reflectors enable direct surface disinfection where the reflectors focus UV light sources onto the surface to be disinfected.

Potential advantages of using UVGI for room disinfection are:

- Automated process that can be validated.
- Improved cleaning efficiency by reducing the need for manual cleaning.
- Better assurance to reach hard to reach surfaces.
- No hazardous chemicals involved.
- Relatively quick process where minimal room preparation is required.

However, care must also be taken when selecting UV light due to the long exposure times required and the problems of poor penetration.

Hydrogen Peroxide Vapour (HPV) Decontamination

With hydrogen peroxide decontamination, 30-35% w/w aqueous hydrogen peroxide is vaporised within the area to be decontaminated. Hydrogen peroxide vapour (HPV) is an oxidising agent and when it comes into contact with microorganisms, the cells or spores are oxidised and inactivated. HPV is generated and distributed within the area ensuring distribution to all parts of the room. At dew point, the saturated HPV in the environment forms a micro-condensation on all exposed surfaces and hence deactivates microorganisms.

HPV can target hard to reach and access areas, however, areas that are not exposed to HPV will not be disinfected. Presence of organic matter or soil reduces the efficacy of HPC. Therefore the surfaces will need to be prepared to remove soiling. HPV is a hazardous chemical and there are strict health and safety exposure limits associated with its use. Because of this reason, HPV decontamination can only be used in unoccupied areas where access to the area of decontamination is not accessible during the process. A thorough health and safety risk assessment is required before carrying out decontamination using HPV. Another consideration is that HPV will trigger fire alarms and prior to the start of the decontamination process, the relevant fire alarms need to be isolated.

Potential advantages of HPV decontamination:

- Log six reduction of bioburden is possible.
- Automated process .
- Useful intervention during outbreak of infections or newly commissioned clinical area.
- Evidence to support its use as an adjuvant to routine cleaning.

For further information on HPV, refer to chapter 9.

6.7 Chapter Summary

HCAI and cleanliness of healthcare environment are inseparable. These are key topics and a main focus for national and European targets for improvement. This is because patient safety is at risk. In order to sustain and further improve HCAI in healthcare settings, commitment from all stakeholders is essential. The use of disinfectants and detergents has played a major role in combating HCAI and they will remain fundamental in reducing HCAI rates. There are several technological advances which have been made on area decontamination in the form of UVGI and HPV technology. As more evidence becomes available and the uses of both technologies are more wide spread, these could well be the next step in tackling HCAI.

6.8 References

1. Turner, R. (2008): *Healthcare associated infections stemming risk of superbug*, Kings Fund Briefing, Kings Fund, London
2. Health Protection Agency (2014): *Quarterly Epidemiological commentary: Mandatory MRSA and MSSA bacteraemia, and clostridium difficile infection data up to July – September 2014*
3. Department of Health media centre (2012): *New Year ambitions to reduce healthcare associated infections at: https://www.gov.uk/government/news/new-year-ambitions-to-reduce-healthcare-associated-infections*
4. Department of Health (2011): *Operation Framework for the NHS in England 2012/13*, Department of Health, London
5. Department of Health (2011): *Technical Guidance for the 2012/2013 Operating Framework*, Department of Health, London
6. Health Protection Agency (2008): *Investigation of specimens for screening for MRSA.* National Standard Method BSOP 29 Issue 5.1
7. Health Protection Agency (2008): *Processing of faeces for Clostridium difficile* National Standard Method BSOP 10 Issue 1.3
8. National Health Service, England (2009): SI 2009 No. 660 The Healthcare and Social Care Act 2008 (Registration of Regulated Activities) Regulation 2009
9. National Patient Safety Agency (2009): *The Revised Healthcare Cleaning Manual v 2*, National Health Service, London

10. National Patient Safety Agency (2007): Safer Practice Note No.15: Colour coding hospital cleaning materials and equipment Ref NPSA/ 2007/15, National Health Service, London
11. Department of Health (2007): PL CNO (2007)6: Improving cleanliness and infection control, DoH, London
12. St Georges Healthcare NHS Trust (2008): *Decontamination Policy,* internal document, St Georges Healthcare NHS Trust, London
13. Microbiology Advisory Committee (2013) *Guidance on decontamination and infection control, including surgical instruments, dental equipment, endoscopes and benchtop steam sterilizers,* Medicines and Healthcare products Regulatory Agency and Department of Health, London
14. Medical Device Agency (2005): DB2002 (05) *Decontamination of Endoscopes,* Department of Health, Social Services and Public Safety, Belfast
15. NHS Estates 2013: Health Technical Memorandum HTM2030: Washer Disinfectors, Department of Health, London
16. Working Party Report (2002) *Rinse water for heat labile endoscopy equipment.* The Journal of Hospital Infection. 51 (1): 7-16

CHAPTER 7:

CLEANING AND DISINFECTION PROCEDURES: A CASE STUDY

By Amit Chandra

7.1 Introduction

Contamination control ranks high amongst pharmaceutical manufacturing requirements. It is especially important for products which do not receive terminal sterilisation and are packaged using aseptic filling techniques in clean rooms (1-3). Figure 1 (below) shows the manual cell culture room of the Cell Therapy Manufacturing Facility (CTMF) at the Centre for Biological Engineering at Loughborough University. The facility provides both the physical requirements and technical expertise to aseptically culture, expand, differentiate and harvest human adherent cells to be used for the preparation of GMP compliant batches of somatic cell therapies and tissue engineered products using an automated cell culture platform (4). The steps of manufacturing to avoid contamination are generally always the same within pharmaceutical processing. It is necessary to ensure that (5):

- The input materials are sterile (or clean and disinfect them),
- The manufacturing/processing is performed in clean containers and
- That the packaging is done in a clean environment with a very low airborne particulate count.

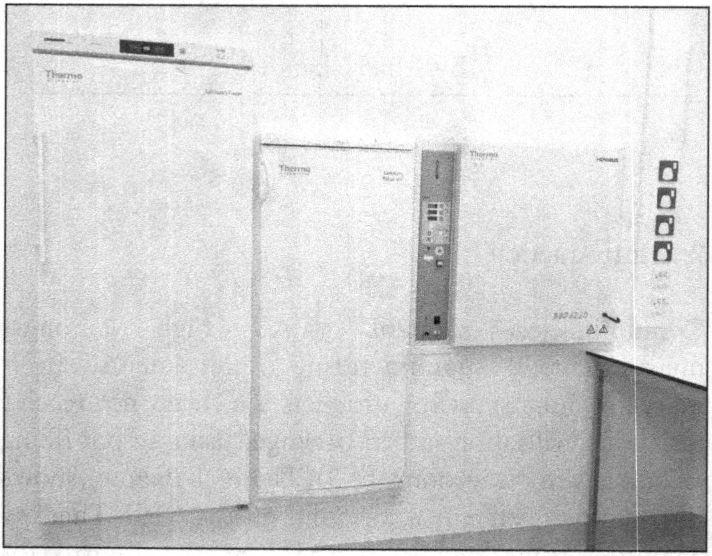

Figure 1: View of the manual cell culture cleanroom at the Cell Therapy Manufacturing Facility (CTMF) at the Centre for Biological Engineering at Loughborough University.

Photograph credited to Vincent Scothern. Copyright with Loughborough University.

Particulates – both viable and non-viable can either enter cleanrooms or are generated within them (6).

Contamination can enter the cleanrooms in fluids and on solids like plasticware, or packaging; or it can be carried on clothing and skin. Particulates can be generated during processing (e.g. friction during handling of plasticware, glassware, and equipment) and during movement of personnel. Small particles (size<10μm) often settle on surfaces and are not easily blown away by the turbulent air flow design found in most cleanrooms.

It is important to remove most particulates in the cleanroom even though they may be larger than any living particles. This is because the living (viable) particulates may settle and grow on the non-viable particulates. Therefore there must be procedures for cleaning and thus removing the majority of the non-viable particulates as well as eliminating the viable particulates by sterilisation. This chapter has been written with a small scale cleanroom operation in mind. Here the process of disinfection and cleaning are often performed together to reduce the workload. In the example work instruction presented at the end of the chapter, the cleaning protocols use disinfectants which are for disinfection purposes. This usage depends on how dirty the surfaces requiring cleaning and disinfecting are (7). The dirtier the surface, the less effective is the process of disinfecting. Disinfectants need to contact the area to disinfect and cannot do this effectively with a barrier of dirt in the way. It is expected that the cleanrooms are maintained in a sufficiently clean state that both cleaning and disinfection can be done together.

The importance of cleaning must be recognised to ensure the quality of pharmaceutical products. This requires that the facility is operated in line with Good Manufacturing Practice (GMP) where specific cleaning practices need to be adopted throughout the facility (8). The effectiveness of all specific cleaning requirements should be subject to validation against written protocols and assessed using validated test methods. The deployment of these cleaning processes should be documented in Cleaning Validation Plans to ensure that contamination risks to products are effectively mitigated. Consideration to cleaning requirements should be given when developing and validating any changes to the facility, equipment or manufacturing processes.

Staff training is essential and a key component of the effectiveness of cleaning and the minimisation of contamination risk to the product. Strict dress codes and changing procedures should be in place and all activities in the facility must be carefully monitored. Only approved materials that have been assessed for the risk they present to the cleanliness of the facility and the risk presented to both the product and the validation status of the cleaning procedures should be permitted into the cleanrooms. Thus, cleaning and disinfection procedures are an amalgamation of the following:

a) Cleaning validation plan which leads to the protocols developed for the validation of the cleaning,
b) Identification of staff and any training requirements for the staff ensure that the training is assessed and records maintained,
c) Schedule of the cleaning and disinfecting operations,
d) Cleaning work instructions and equipment/material to be used.

This chapter will describe each of the above.

7.2 Cleaning validation plan

The cleaning validation plan (CVP) should be set up to comply with the facility quality and regulatory compliance strategy in mind. The CVP defines and documents the key elements for the qualification of the cleaning procedures to be followed in the cleanroom facility once the commissioning has taken place. As part of the validation strategy, the purpose of the CVP is to identify, describe or cross reference the following information:

a) The facility, utilities and equipment systems to be subject to cleaning validation.
b) The general procedures to be validated.
c) The particular potential contaminants to be covered in the validation activities undertaken.
d) The methodology to be used must provide evidence that the cleaning processes have been specified, designed, documented and performed to an agreed scope of work, and in compliance with relevant SOPs.

The CVP should also provide the basis for cleaning validation and quality system activities for GMP compliance, covering all the facility-dedicated systems, which include the premises (the facility itself and the various rooms) and all the equipment accommodated within the facility.

It should be the responsibility of an identified validation steering committee (VSC) to approve the document and to monitor and approve the execution of the validation plan. The job functions and responsibilities of personnel executing the activities should be defined in the relevant validation protocol. Any person performing validation exercises in relation to the CVP document should be trained to the standard required. Any person operating equipment or processes in relation to the CVP document should be trained to the relevant procedure and should hold documented evidence within their personal training record. All equipment, services and processes should be subject to change control in accordance with the facility change control system. This is particularly useful to maintain the validation status when there are any changes.

The validation plan for the facility is normally based on an assessment of the contamination and cross contamination risk assessment. This assessment identifies the routes of contamination as having direct impact, indirect impact or no impact on product quality in line with the guidance provided by ISPE 'Baseline™ Guide to Commissioning and Qualification' (9). The effectiveness of the cleaning procedures approved for the facility should be demonstrated by comparing the data from particulate monitoring (viable and non-viable) of the facility for a period of time before and after a full clean. This is primarily undertaken by assessing the levels of microorganisms recovered from surfaces using swabs and contact plates. The post cleaning survey of bioburden levels is collected from a broad range of locations by a variety of methods. Often the sampling plans will depend upon an initial Installation Qualification data set which also determines sampling plans in accordance with a risk based approach for further operational qualification. The effectiveness of cleaning and disinfection is undertaken by comparing the microbial count levels from the surface monitoring pre and post-cleaning and noting the reduction. In addition, an assessment of the microorganisms recovered should be made so that any potentially resistant strains can be noted (10).

All facilities define their equipment in the installation qualification. The equipment identified should also be subject to specific validation protocols that will confirm the effectiveness of the documented cleaning procedures to ensure that surface particulates, residual cleaning agents and bioburden levels meet the specified requirements.

The validation of materials and equipment for specific processes should be documented in specific process validation documentation prior to execution of that process.

7.3 Staff Identification and Training Requirement

All staff working within the cleanroom facility must be identified and records maintained on the staff training. Any contracted staff for the facility providing services to the facility having an impact on product quality, validated status or quality system operation must be assessed and their training documented. As cleaning of the cleanrooms will have an effect on the product quality and thus impact the status of the facility, all external cleaning crews must have their training assessed and recorded.

It is the responsibility of the Technical Lead and Project Management to ensure that all staff have access to appropriate training to enable them to fulfil the roles assigned to them. It is the responsibility of all staff within the facility to ensure they do not undertake any task or activity for which they have not completed and documented training. The main tasks to maintain training records are:

a) Each member of staff should have a job description for their role(s) in the cleanroom facility.
b) Each member of staff should be responsible for ensuring that they have the appropriate training and have read the current procedures appropriate to the roles identified on their job description.
c) Each member of staff should have an individual training record that will identify what, when and as appropriate the result of all training activities undertaken. This record should also identify where a requirement is satisfied by experience.
d) Where appropriate, training activities should be followed by a documented assessment of competency that is included in the staff member's training record.
e) Additional evidence of training (course certificates) or experience (edited curricula vitae) should be kept with the training records as appropriate.
f) A central file detailing the relevant experience and qualifications of all contract staff should be maintained. This should include, where appropriate, specific training records against facility procedures and work instructions (e.g. Entry to cleanrooms, cleaning of surfaces etc.).

7.4 Cleaning Schedules

Clear instructions must be provided for the cleaning schedule to be followed for the cleanroom facility and the documentation to be completed to record the cleaning undertaken. This may reference a series of work instructions that provide step by step instructions for the cleaning of the cleanroom facility and its equipment. The applied frequencies and areas of application are best determined by risk assessment.

This risk assessment is performed to document the risks to product quality presented by sources of contamination and to identify the potential transfer route of this contamination. The document assesses the risk and the effect of steps taken to mitigate and minimise this risk. In a typical risk assessment, cleaning procedures will be used to mitigate many of the risks like the contamination of surfaces by people, material transfer, air movements etc.

The first step in deciding the cleaning frequency is to classify the facility into three areas:

a) Critical areas (i.e., production areas or directly adjacent, e.g., operations room, cryo-storage room).
b) General areas (i.e., areas which are in the cleanroom facility and are maintained with a low particulate count by the air handling regime e.g., change rooms, consumables cupboards).
c) Other areas (i.e., areas which are outside the primary facility e.g., bulk store rooms, cold store rooms which are not maintained in the same air handling regime).

Surfaces in each of the three areas can be cleaned at different frequencies depending upon their proximity to

Ease of dispersion or transfer of contamination						
	4	High frequency of contact with potential contaminants	Established cleaning processes applied weekly	Validated cleaning processes applied daily	Fully validated cleaning processes prior to use	Fully validated cleaning processes immediately prior to use
	3	Frequent contact with potential contaminants	Monthly cleaning to approved cleaning processes	Validated cleaning processes applied daily	Fully validated cleaning processes prior to use	Fully validated cleaning processes immediately prior to use
	2	Moderate contact with potential contaminants	Monthly cleaning to documented processes	Established cleaning processes applied weekly	Fully validated cleaning processes prior to use	Fully validated cleaning processes immediately prior to use
	1	Negligible contact with potential contaminants	Quarterly cleaning to documented processes	Established cleaning processes applied weekly	Validated cleaning processes applied daily	Fully validated cleaning processes prior to use
			Minimal risk of contact or transfer to product	Potential for transfer to product	Risk of contact or transfer to product	Direct Product Contact
			1	2	3	4
			Proximity of source to critical area			

Figure 2. Matrix used to quantify the risk level for each piece of equipment and to identify the level of cleaning validation and cleaning processes required. The colour coding is used in the room assessment tables to identify the required level of cleaning. Specific cleaning work instructions detail the actual procedures to be followed.

the critical areas and the ease of dispersion or transfer of contaminants. The surfaces of equipment are also included in this risk mitigation strategy. Figure 2 shows a matrix which can be used to define the cleaning frequency:

The cleaning should be planned on a facility calendar by the facility manager in accordance with the following schedules decided. The calendar shall also note which disinfectant is to be used to maintain the requirements for disinfectant rotation (rotation between disinfectants of different modes of activity is an EU GMP requirement).

It is necessary to note that the cleaning schedule represents the minimum frequency of cleaning required and additional cleaning operations may be instigated as a result of specific events (e.g. spillage, specific critical manufacturing processes, external contamination and introduction of new equipment). Also more frequent cleaning may be required in periods of high humidity or high staff occupancy and activity levels.

7.5 Cleaning Work Instruction, Materials and Equipment

Clear operating procedures and work instructions are required for each cleaning activity in the cleanroom facility. An example work instruction for a "critical" room is presented in this part of the chapter. This work instruction provides step by step instructions that are to be followed when cleaning the surfaces in a cleanroom facility of a room which is close to the product. It should be one of a series of work instructions controlling the general cleanliness of the cleanroom suite and thus reducing the chances of contamination and cross contamination of products. This work instruction deals with the key responsibilities of the staff, health and safety issues, equipment and materials, procedures for cleaning the room and equipment, disposal of waste materials and record keeping.

a) Key Responsibilities

Under this heading, the work instruction defines the key personnel who are involved in the cleaning of the cleanroom facility. The Facility Manager is responsible for ensuring that all staff cleaning the cleanroom facility are trained against this work instruction and are authorised to access the cleanroom suite. All personnel cleaning the CTMF cleanroom suite are responsible for ensuring they comply with the practices and importantly the sequence of actions as detailed in this instruction.

b) Health and Safety

All staff must follow safe practices according to (11) safety risk assessments for the handling and disposal of the cleaning materials used in this work instruction. Under this heading, all risk assessments should be referenced.

c) Equipment/Materials

All equipment and cleaning agents to be used in the cleaning of the facility should be defined and listed. It is also useful to have the item code or part number of the consumables which helps in the re-ordering. Examples of what products are required are as follows:

a. List of all the disinfectants to be used in liquid form (preferably two or more for rotation purposes). It is often good practice to have disinfectants which do not cause metal parts to rust especially for equipment surfaces. These disinfectants are kept separate from the ones for walls and ceilings. The disinfectant can be in the form of a liquid and dry wipes or impregnated wipes.
b. The alcohol preparation which is used as a disinfectant in the form of liquid and dry wipes or impregnated wipes.
c. Neutral detergent in the form of liquid and dry wipes or impregnated wipes
d. Any mop heads, buckets, waste bags and ties.

d) Procedure

The work instruction for the cleaning procedure is necessarily prescriptive. This is to ensure that all staff performing the cleaning operations are performing the same procedure and in the same order. In the sample work instruction provided below, the procedure refers to the preparation of equipment, cleaning of the ceiling and upper walls, cleaning of stationary equipment, cleaning of non-stationary equipment, cleaning of walls, cleaning of the floor, and for the removal of disinfectant residues.

Preparation of equipment and consumables

This subsection addresses the locations of all the cleaning material and the checks required before cleaning commences. All required equipment and cleaning products should be located in identified places in the store room, flammables cabinet, or corrosives cabinet etc. The steps to prepare equipment and consumables are:

- Check the Cleaning Schedule to confirm the cleaning products to be used and the rooms and surfaces to be cleaned.
- Check that all cleaning products are within expiry date.
- Cleaning and Room Entry: Comply with appropriate dress code and entry procedures for each area being accessed for cleaning. (NB: Safety goggles and face masks are required to protect the face from dripping products)
- Clean the rooms in strict sequence from highest classification to lowest classification and from furthest point from entry to nearest.
- Clean all the identified areas according to the cleaning schedule.
- Clean all identified areas working from highest point to lowest point (e.g. ceilings, walls, work surfaces, floors).
- Clean all rooms starting at the end of the room furthest from the exit.
- Transfer cleaning materials between rooms using the appropriate material transfer hatches and appropriate cleaning of packaging.
- Secure waste generated from the cleaning procedure in suitable waste bags and remove via waste transfer hatches.
- Document all cleaning activities on the prescribed cleaning log sheet.

Cleaning the Ceilings and Upper Third of Walls

The steps involved are:

a) Start by using dry wipes and prepare the solution in the bucket and generate wet wipes. Alternatively, if using sterile disinfectant impregnated mop wipes, place the mop wipes on the mop heads but always remember to check the shelf-life of the pre-impregnated mop wipes.
b) Ensure that you have face mask and safety goggles to protect against drips from mop heads.
c) Using overlapping mop strokes, wipe down the ceiling and upper third of the walls, working methodically around the area starting at the furthest reach point and working from the corners towards yourself in a straight line. Replace the mop wipe if the wipe becomes visibly contaminated or dries out.

NOTE 1: Particular attention should be paid to corners and edges where yarn mops may be used.

NOTE 2: Particular attention should be paid to HVAC grilles and vents using impregnated hand wipes.

Cleaning of Stationary Equipment in the rooms

The steps for cleaning stationary equipment in the cleanrooms are:

a) Complete the cleaning instruction for each piece of equipment according to the work instructions and cleaning schedule.

b) Cleaning External Surfaces of Stationary Equipment.
c) Use disinfectant impregnated low particulate wipes (use the disinfectant which does allow metallic surfaces to rust).
d) Using one clean disinfectant impregnated low particulate wipe for each piece of equipment wipe down all external surfaces using overlapping strokes.
e) When wiping down work methodically around area starting at the furthest reach point and work towards yourself using overlapping strokes and starting at the top and working downwards. Particular attention should be paid to corners and edges. Replace the wipe when the wipe is visibly contaminated or dry.

Cleaning External Surfaces of Non-Stationary Equipment

Non stationary equipment includes (but not limited to) trolleys, waste bins and containers, utensils, cleanroom furniture and ladders. The steps are:

a) Use disinfectant impregnated low particulate wipes (those which do not cause rusting).
b) Using one clean sterile disinfectant impregnated low particulate wipe, for each piece of equipment wipe down all external surfaces using overlapping strokes.
c) When wiping down work methodically around area starting at the furthest reach point and work towards yourself ensuring overlapping strokes. Particular attention should be paid to undersides, corners and edges. Replace the wipe when it is visibly contaminated or dirty.

Walls and other Vertical Surfaces

Cleaning under this sub heading includes doors, door handles, windows, stepovers, underside of benches and work tops, electrical trunking, wall mounted equipment such as grilles, dispensers, intercoms, mirrors and hooks. Dry mop wipes wetted with disinfectant should be used on large flat surfaces. Impregnated hand wipes or yarn mops should be used for small items, irregular surfaces or edges (e.g. grilles, door frames) or around high risk areas, such as door handles, electrical trunking, intercoms etc., following the wipe procedure. The steps are as follows:

a) If using dry wipes, prepare the solution in the bucket and wet the wipes. Use the mop wipe wetted with disinfectant and mops for the large areas.
b) Using overlapping mop strokes, wipe down the walls, doors, windows or other large vertical surfaces, working methodically around the area starting at furthest reach point and working from the corners in straight vertical lines towards the floor. Replace the mop wipe if the wipe becomes visibly contaminated.

NOTE 1: Particular attention should be paid to corners and edges, yarn mops may be used.

NOTE 2: Particular attention should be paid to HVAC grilles and vents.

Cleaning Work Surfaces and other Horizontal Surfaces.

Cleaning in this sub heading includes transfer hatches. The steps are:

a) Using one clean disinfectant impregnated low particulate wipe, for each work surface wipe down using overlapping strokes.
b) When wiping down work methodically around the area starting at the furthest reach point and work towards yourself in a straight line ensuring overlapping strokes. Particular attention should be paid to corners and edges. Replace the wipe when all areas of the wipe are visibly contaminated.
c) Clean both sides of transfer hatch doors from within the room. Internal hatch surfaces should be cleaned after removal of waste and from the lowest classification or latest room cleaned in this sequence.

Removal of disinfectant residues.

The steps to remove the disinfectant are:

a) Leave the disinfectant solution on the surface for the manufacturer's recommended contact time (such as for a minimum of 5 minutes, or as directed) to allow the disinfectant to be effective.
b) Fit second mop head with mop wipes impregnated with alcohol (e.g. isopropyl alcohol or Ethanol-Propanol blend).
c) Using the fresh mop head wipe down ceiling and upper third of wall using overlapping mop strokes to remove any residue, working methodically around the area starting at the furthest reach point and working from the corners towards yourself in a straight line. Replace the mop wipe if the wipe becomes visibly contaminated or dry.
d) Open the pack of sterile impregnated alcohol wipes for hand cleaning on surfaces to remove any residues.

e) When wiping down work methodically around the area starting at the furthest reach point and work towards yourself ensuring overlapping strokes and starting at the top and working downwards. Particular attention should be paid to corners and edges.
f) Windows and mirrors may be additionally wiped separately to ensure clarity neutral detergent wipes or mop wipes.
g) Discard all used alcohol mop wipes and alcohol wipes to waste.

Cleaning of Floors

The steps for cleaning the floors are:

a) Either roll all of the floor surfaces with a tacky roller to remove any loose debris and fibres, moving any equipment to one half of the room nearest the exit door, or wipe the floor using a neutral detergent solution and mop and bucket.
b) Use a mop with a ready prepared disinfectant solution (alternatively a disinfectant impregnated mop wipe could be used, but always check the shelf life).
c) Using overlapping mop strokes, wipe down half the floor area, working methodically around the area starting at furthest reach point and working towards yourself in a straight line. Replace the mop wipe if the wipe becomes visibly contaminated or dry.
d) NOTE: Particular attention should be paid to corners and edges.
e) Leave the disinfectant solution on the surface for the manufacturer's recommended contact time to allow the disinfectant to be effective.

f) Remove the mop head and discard to waste.
g) Fit a second mop head wetted with a ready prepared alcohol solution (e.g. isopropyl alcohol or Ethanol-Propanol blend). Alternatively a disinfectant impregnated mop wipe could be used, but always check the shelf life.
h) After the allotted time, using the fresh mop head wipe down using overlapping mop strokes to remove any residue, working methodically around the area starting at the furthest reach point and working towards yourself in a straight line. Replace the mop wipe if the wipe becomes visibly contaminated or dry.
i) Move equipment to the cleaned floor area ensuring that contact surfaces are wiped prior to being replaced on the clean surface.
j) Repeat steps for the other half of the floor area.

e) Disposal of Waste Materials

After any cleaning activity, dispose of waste materials in waste bags and seal. Waste bags should be removed from the cleanroom suite via waste hatches. The bags should be disposed of in accordance with appropriate facility waste management procedures.

f) Documents

The key documents which require completing after the cleaning activity are:

- Cleanroom entry logbook,
- Cleaning Records.

7.6 Conclusion

Information in this chapter has been taken from the current approach for cleaning at the Cell Therapy Manufacturing Facility. This chapter has presented a holistic approach to developing cleaning and disinfecting procedures. It takes into consideration the validation plan and the protocols for the validation of the cleaning. The chapter also includes a summary of the requirements for staff training and training records and has a guide to help develop a schedule for cleaning a facility. The chapter ends with a framework of a work instruction for cleaning a "critical" room in the cleanroom facility and all the equipment in the room. The work instruction includes a choice of cleaning products, the method for disinfecting using disinfectants and then wiping away the residue to reduce the viable particle count level.

7.7 References and Further Reading:

1. ISO 14644 series – Cleanrooms and associated controlled environments, International Standards Organisation, Geneva, Switzerland.
2. IEST-RP-CC018.4–2007 Cleanroom Housekeeping: Operating and Monitoring Procedures, Institute of Environmental Sciences and Technology, Arlington Heights, Illinois, USA.
3. IEST-RP-CC023.2-2006 Microorganisms in Cleanrooms, Institute of Environmental Sciences and Technology, Arlington Heights, Illinois, USA.
4. Website for the Centre for Biological Engineering, Loughborough University, online at: http://www.lboro.ac.uk/lcbe, accessed on 29 February 2012.
5. Cooper, D. W. (1996) Cleaning Aseptic Fill Areas, *Pharmaceutical Technology*, 20(2), 52–60.
6. Whyte, W. (2010) Cleanroom Technology, Chichester, John Wiley & Sons.
7. Sandle, T. (2014) Selection and use of Cleaning and Disinfection Agents in Pharmaceutical Manufacturing. In Handlon, G. and Sandle, T. (Eds.) *Industrial Pharmaceutical Microbiology: Standards & Controls,* Euromed Communications, Passfield, UK, 9.1–9.32
8. Euradlex. The Rules Governing Medicinal Products in the European Community (2009), Annex 1, published by the European Commission, Brussels, Belgium.
9. ISPE (2002) 'Baseline™ Guide to Commissioning and Qualification', International Society for Pharmaceutical Engineering, Volume 5, Tampa, Florida, USA.

10. Vina, P., Rubio, S. and Sandle, T. (2011): 'Selection and Validation of Disinfectants', in Saghee, M.R., Sandle, T. and Tidswell, E.C. (Eds.) (2011): Microbiology and Sterility Assurance in Pharmaceuticals and Medical Devices, New Delhi: Business Horizons, pp219-236.
11. Regulations and Guidance on Control of Substances Hazardous to Health (COSHH), Health and Safety Executive, London, UK online at: http://www.hse.gov.uk/coshh/accessed on 29 February 2012.

CHAPTER 8:

APPLICATION OF DISINFECTANTS AND DETERGENTS IN THE PHARMACEUTICAL SECTOR

By Tim Sandle

8.1 Introduction

Cleanrooms, as controlled environments, are required for the manufacture of pharmaceutical products. Cleanrooms are assigned a class (through ISO 14644) or a grade (as per EU GMP) through meeting a set standard for the concentration of airborne particles. However once a grade is assigned a series of other physical and microbial parameters must be met. Other requirements include readily cleanable surfaces. Floors, walls, and ceilings must have smooth, non-porous surfaces. Furthermore, particulate, temperature, and humidity controls need to be defined and adhered to. In addition, cleaning and disinfecting procedures are required so that microbial cleanliness can be maintained.

The physical parameters controlled through Heating Ventilation and Air Conditioning Systems (HVAC), with particulate cleanliness achieved through the use of air filters: HEPA (High Efficiency Particulate Air) or ULPA (ultra-low penetration air). The inner part of the HEPA / ULPA filters is designed to capture particles as they pass through in the moving air stream. Due to these physical functions most cleanrooms, when unoccupied, meet cleanliness standards. People, however, are the primary source of contamination in cleanrooms. This means that when cleanrooms are occupied the most significant contamination risks can arise. Cleanliness is maintained through control of personnel and through robust cleaning and disinfection programmes. This chapter is concerned with these programmes and their application within the pharmaceutical sector.

An effective cleaning and disinfection programme in pharmaceutical grade areas of a Good Manufacturing Practice (GMP) facility is critical to assure the quality of the products. It is not sufficient to simply have a programme in place for regulatory agencies require validation data to support sanitisation and disinfection procedures. For example, the FDA Guideline for Aseptic Processing states, "the suitability, efficacy, and limitations of disinfecting agents and procedures should be assessed. The effectiveness of these disinfectants and procedures should be measured by their ability to ensure that potential contaminants are adequately removed from surfaces".

The focus of the chapter is upon the regulations and procedural requirements.

The chapter examines the following:

- Why detergents and disinfectants are used in pharmaceutical grade cleanrooms
- The requirement for disinfectant rotation
- The use of detergents and disinfectants in aseptic processing areas
- The importance of compatibility trials
- The need to conduct field trial validation
- The assessment of disinfectant performance and cleaning techniques using microbiological environmental monitoring
- The key points for a cleaning and disinfection protocol and policy.

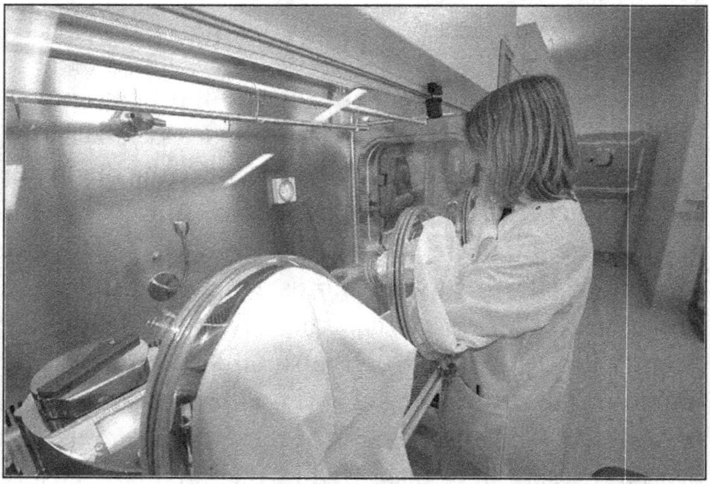

Figure 1: An isolator within a pharmaceutical grade cleanroom (© Tim Sandle)

8.2 Detergents and disinfectants

Disinfectant solutions are chemical or physical agents that destroy or remove vegetative forms of harmful microorganisms when applied to a surface. Several chapters in this book have detailed what detergents and disinfectants are and the key criteria for their selection (refer to chapter one for the basic concepts). The types of disinfectants selected must be effective for use within cleanrooms and must be controlled (1).

To conform with GMP expectations, pharmaceutical manufacturers are expected to use at least two disinfectants with different modes of activity (2). Whilst the two disinfectants do not need to be sporicidal, the use of a sporicidal disinfectant is recommended for aseptic processing areas, at least on an occasional basis, even where such a disinfectant does not form part of the standard set. Therefore, a third disinfectant is often held in reserve and deployed at a lower frequency to the two primary disinfectants.

8.3 Regulatory expectations

The use of detergents and disinfectants, and the need to keep cleanrooms clean, is a regulatory requirement within the pharmaceutical sector. The main regulatory documents relating to the use of disinfectants in pharmaceutical manufacturing are:

- FDA Code of Federal Regulations: 21 CFR 211.56b and 21 CFR 211.56c (which refer to sanitation); CFR 211.67 (which refer to equipment and maintenance); CFR 211.182 (which describes the need for a cleaning programme); and CFR 211.113b
- FDA Aseptic Processing Guide, revised 2004
- USP (General Chapter <1072> Disinfectants and Antiseptics)

- Annex 1 to the EU Guide to Good Manufacturing Practice

For example, the 21 CFR 211.67 states:

That surfaces and equipment must be "....cleaned, maintained, and sanitized at appropriate intervals to prevent malfunctions or contamination that would alter the safety, identity, strength, quality, or purity of the drug product beyond the official or other established requirements".

Figure 2: Cleaning a cleanroom, using the triple bucket system, within a pharmaceutical cleanroom (© Tim Sandle)

To meet regulatory expectations in the pharmaceutical industry, a cleaning and disinfection programme is required. The programme should consist of a policy, outlining the objectives and the criteria for the selection of materials and cleaning agents; and a procedure, detailing how cleaning is undertaken, along with the techniques and cleaning frequencies. There is an expectation that such programmes are regularly reviewed and reflect any changes to cleanroom design and respond to changes in environmental monitoring data.

Although there are some differences between the regulations, a number of similar areas are covered. In summary, the regulations require:

- The need to have written procedures (CFR / EU GMP).
- Responsibilities for cleaning should be assigned (CFR). Often this is interpreted as the need to have independent cleaning staff separate from those involved in product manufacture.
- Staff must be trained in cleaning techniques and have a training record (CFR/EU GMP).
- Details of cleaning frequencies, methods, equipment and materials must be recorded in written procedures (CFR). This may relate to an approved supplier specification.
- The cleaning of equipment and materials must take place at regular intervals (CFR)
- In designing a disinfectant protocol for the sanitisation of floors, walls and surfaces, a pharmaceutical organisation will normally select two or three disinfectants for the same application. This is a requirement of regulatory bodies and the strongest pressure for it has come from Europe with the EU GMP

Guide stating that "where disinfectants are used, more than one type should be employed" (Annex 1, paragraph 3714). This is normally interpreted as the need for disinfectant rotation (which is discussed below).

- Disinfectants should be rotated (EU GMP / FDA warning letters).
- Inspection of equipment for cleanliness before use should be part of routine operations (CFR).
- A cleaning log should be kept. The purpose is to keep a record of the areas cleaned, agents used and the identity of the operator (CFR).
- The microorganisms isolated (the 'microflora') from environmental monitoring programmes should be examined for resistant strains (EU GMP). The inference here is that such isolates are incorporated into disinfectant efficacy studies (see chapter ten).
- The monitoring for microbial contamination in disinfectant and detergent solutions should be periodically undertaken (EU GMP)
- The storing of disinfectant and detergent solutions should be for defined [and short] periods (EU GMP)
- Disinfectants and detergents used in EU GMP Grade A and B/ISO 14644 class 5 and 7 in operation cleanrooms should be sterile before use (EU GMP)
- Room use should be recorded after each operation (CFR / EU GMP)
- Disinfectants should be 'qualified' (validated) (CFR)
- There should be a technical agreement with the company who supplies the disinfectant. Ideally the disinfectants purchased should be lot tracked (EU GMP).

8.4 Environmental cleanliness standards

Pharmaceutical grade cleanrooms are either assigned a grade (as with EU or WHO GMP) or a class (through the international cleanroom standard ISO 14644). The FDA use ISO 14644 classes. The grade or class is based on the cleanliness of airborne particulates and should conform to the intended use of the room. For EU GMP two cumulative particle count sizes are measured to assess cleanliness: 0.5 µm and 5.0 µm; whereas, for the FDA requirements, only measurement of the 0.5 µm size is required.

A comparison between EU GMP (3) and ISO 14644 (4), for when cleanrooms are 'at rest' (not occupied) and 'in operation', is shown in the table below:

		At Rest		
		0.5 µm		5.0 µm
Grade	Annex 1	ISO 14644-1 (Class) Count	Annex 1	ISO 14644-1 (Class) Count
A	3,520	(5) 3,520	20	5 20
B	3,520	(5) 3,520	29	(5) 29
C	352,000	(7) 352,000	2,900	(7) 2,930
D	3,520,00	(8) 3,520,000	29,000	(8) 29, 300
		Operational		
		0.5 µm		5.0 µm
Grade	Annex 1	ISO 14644-1 (Class) Count	Annex 1	ISO 14644-1 (Class) Count
A	3,520	(5) 3,520	20	5 20
B	352,000	(7) 352,000	2,900	(7) 2,930
C	3,520,000	(8) 3,520,000	29,000	(8) 29,300
D	Not Defined		Not Defined	

Table 1: Table of particulate limits for EU GMP and ISO 14644

Typical room uses are:

- Grade A: The local zone for high risk operations, e.g. filling zone, stopper bowls, open ampoules and vials, making aseptic connections. Normally such conditions are provided by a unidirectional air flow device, providing a homogeneous air speed in a range of 0.36 – 0.54 m/s at the working position in open cleanroom applications.
- Grade B: For aseptic preparation and filling, this is the background environment for the Grade A zone.
- Grade C and D: Clean areas for carrying out less critical stages in the manufacture of sterile products. With Grade C, this includes the preparation of solutions to be filtered. With Grade D this includes the handling of components after washing.

Cleaning and disinfection programmes in pharmaceutical facilities are designed to keep the numbers of microorganisms found on cleanroom surfaces under control. This means through an environmental monitoring programme, where assigned action levels are used to assess the numbers of microorganisms recovered. These numbers are defined in regulatory documents. The two most important documents are EU GMP and FDA guidelines for aseptic processing facilities. For non-aseptic processing areas, the guidelines provide some guidance as towards the appropriate levels. Non-sterile pharma generally set alert and action levels based on an historical review of microbiological data.

These EU GMP levels for surfaces, with air monitoring levels shown for reference, are:

EU GMP

(The Rules Governing Medicinal Products in the European Union: Volume 4 EU Guidelines to Good Manufacturing Practice Medicinal Products for Human and Veterinary Use - Annex 1 Manufacture of Sterile Medicinal Products) (3)

Grade	Air sample (CFU/m^3)	Settle plate (CFU/4 hours)	Contact plates* (diameter 55 mm) CFU/plate
A	<1	<1	<1
B	10	5	5
C	100	50	25
D	200	100	50

* Swabs are not defined. However, the action level for the contact plate is normally taken.

Table 2: Table displaying EU GMP limits for environmental monitoring

8.5 Selection and purchasing

Whilst this chapter has introduced the concepts for the selection of disinfectants, there are steps which the pharmaceutical manufacturer should go through when selecting, specifying and purchasing disinfectants.

A User Requirement Specification (URS) should be drawn up. A URS addresses the questions of what we want to use something for (in this case a disinfectant), how we want to use it, and what restrictions may apply to its use. The URS should cover:

- Specifying the disinfectant.
- Stating where the disinfectant is to be used, for example, in Grade A/B sterile manufacturing areas or in general factory corridors.
- Specifying the range of surfaces that the disinfectant is intended to be used on, such as stainless steel, vinyl, terrazzo and so on. This is important as some disinfectants corrode or discolour particular materials.
- The URS should identify if the disinfectant is to be used alone or in combination with a detergent.
- All health and safety considerations should be identified.
- Environmental protection considerations should be noted.
- The type of presentation should be stated: spray bottles or concentrate, impregnated wipes or mops and so forth.
- Whether a sterile disinfectant is required should be considered.
- What is required from the supplier should be established, in terms of samples, availability for audit, Certificates of Analysis, and where necessary compliance with a Quality System Standard such as IS 9000.
- The pharmaceutical organisation should consider what the supplier should provide in terms of validation documentation.

8.6 Rotation of Disinfectants

Within Europe, the rotation between two disinfectants of differing modes of activity is a regulatory expectation.

The argument for rotating two disinfectants is to reduce the possibility of resistant strains of microorganisms developing. Whilst the phenomenon of microbial resistance is an issue of major concern for antibiotics there are few studies which support development of resistance to disinfectants (5). Resistance is unlikely to develop when disinfectants are applied to dry environments, such as cleanrooms, for microbial replication, as the primary process for gaining resistance, is minimal (6). The requirement for rotation is not as strong within the USA, as the USP general information chapter <1072> "Disinfectants and Antiseptics" states:

> "The development of microbial resistance to antibiotics is a well-described phenomenon. The development of microbial resistance is less likely, as disinfectants are more powerful biocidal agents than antibiotics and are applied in high concentrations against low populations of microorganisms, so the selective pressure for the development of resistance is less profound."

Building immunity to a disinfectant has never been documented in the cleanroom. Most reports of developed resistance are due to inadequate cleaning, improper use of the disinfectant, or poor application of the disinfectant to the surface for a specified contact time. Furthermore antibiotics and disinfectants have different modes of action (with the former targeting specific sites and the latter typically having multiple modes of action). In short, there is no scientific evidence to support disinfectant resistance (7).

Nonetheless, rotation is a requirement needed to satisfy European regulators and if applying it, then it is logical that the disinfectants used for rotation will have differing modes of activity (8). Policies for determining the frequency of rotation vary widely. Some facilities have adopted an even rotation (such as alternating between disinfectants daily or weekly) while others rotate at different frequencies, sometimes to an extreme of three months for one disinfectant against one week for the alternate disinfectant. Other companies build up a case for only using one disinfectant on a day-to-day basis with a second used very infrequently. In this latter example it is argued that two disinfectants only need to be employed if the environmental monitoring data indicate excursions from set limits and therefore the inference is that the primary disinfectant is not controlling surfaces.

The frequency of rotation needs to be defined by the user and supporting data can be supplied through field trials. When established it is necessary to continue the detergent application between the changes of disinfectant types in order to remove residues. Once set, there may be a requirement to vary the frequencies of use, such as in response to an increase to microbial counts and as part of a formal investigation into a microbiological data deviation.

In addition to rotating between two disinfectants with differing modes of activity, there are occasions when a third 'reserve' disinfectant should be considered. A third disinfectant might be applied in circumstances where there is a major contamination event, or the suspected development of a resistant strain, and under circumstances where the two primary disinfectants and any improvement to cleaning techniques or increases to cleaning frequencies do not appear to be effective. Sometimes the third disinfectant is used in a vapour phase to 'gas' the cleanroom (an example is hydrogen peroxide). A case where this might be considered is following cleanroom maintenance.

8.7 Undertaking cleaning and disinfection in pharmaceutical families

The techniques of cleaning and disinfection are important. It does not matter how effective the purchased detergents and disinfectants are unless they are used in the correct way. Otherwise areas will not be cleaned effectively and unduly high levels of microbial contamination will remain.

Order of cleaning and disinfection

The phrase "cleaning and disinfection" not only distinguishes between cleaning agents and disinfectant, it also describes the order in which surfaces are treated. In order for a disinfectant to work effectively, 'soil' (such as grease and dust particles) must be removed first using a suitable cleanroom grade detergent.

Treatment of detergents and disinfectants

An important consideration for application of cleaning agents is whether sterile chemicals are required (this is normally by filtration using a filter with a porosity of

0.45 μm). Normally, agents for use in GMP Grade A and B / ISO class 5 and 7 (dynamic) environments must be sterile, whereas agents for use in GMP Grade C and D / ISO class 8 (in operation) environments are not normally required to be sterile. However, with such lower grade areas it is recommended that the solutions should be qualified or periodically monitored for microbiological contamination and a time limit imposed on how long in-use dilutions be used for and controls in place so that in-use dilutions are discarded after use.

Preparation of detergents and disinfectants

When cleaning and disinfecting large areas, like cleanrooms, ready-to-use solutions of cleaning agents are not often available and instead concentrates of cleaning reagents need to be prepared.

Detergents

The application of a detergent solution, made in hot purified water (when hot water is needed this is normally >25°C), is the primary method of cleaning and removing particulate matter from floors and surfaces in cleanrooms. In some areas, such as an aseptic filling area, hot water is unlikely to be available due to the restriction of water in such areas in order to maintain contamination control. Instead it is more common for detergents to be prepared using Water-for-Injections and filtered through a 0.22 μm filter into the filling area.

It is important that the correct amount of detergent, as defined by the manufacturer's recommendation, is added to the appropriate quantity of purified water. Once prepared, detergents should have defined holding times from preparation to last usage.

Disinfectants

When preparing disinfectant concentrates as ready-to-use solutions the correct amount of disinfectant, as defined by the manufacturer's recommendation, must be added to the appropriate quantity of purified water or Water for Injections. For most disinfectants, hard water is not suitable for use as a diluent. This is because the ions in the water which cause hardness, such as magnesium and calcium, will cause interference with certain active ingredients in the disinfectant formulation. The water added should be of the correct temperature. If the water is too hot, it will cause certain disinfectants to be unstable (such as hydrogen peroxide, which becomes unstable if the water added is at a temperature of 60°C or greater). A temperature range of 20-25°C is suitable for most types of disinfectants (and thus is close to the temperature at which validation of disinfectants is commonly performed, as outlined in chapter ten).

Like detergent solutions, disinfectants should have defined times between preparation and usage. This is either a time applied to disinfectants prepared 'In-house', or the addition of an expiry time to pre-prepared disinfectants. For pre-prepared disinfectants (wipes, trigger sprays and hand sanitisers) the expiry time is often for no more than one month after opening unless supporting data from the manufacturer is available.

Cleaning materials

For disinfectants and detergents used for floors, surfaces and walls these agents should be applied using non-particle shedding, cleanroom certified mop heads, cloths and wipes. These should be of a non-woven, non-particle shedding and lint-free variety (typically a hydro entangled polyester/cellulose blend), ideally with a large liquid holding capacity. For surfaces in Grade A / ISO class 5 and Grade B / ISO class 7 cleanrooms the solutions should be applied using certified cleanroom mop heads, cloths and wipes.

The wipes used should be effective at removing non-viable particulates, capable of applying a disinfectant, and capable of the subsequent removal of viable contamination. It is also important the wipe does not contribute to the bioburden or generate additional particulates. Transfer of such materials into an aseptic area should include an adequate decontamination step (for example, irradiated mop heads which have been multiple-wrapped). Similarly, buckets used for the application of detergents or disinfectants, in Grade B / ISO class7 (dynamic) rooms should be autoclaved before use. For Grade C / ISO class 8 and Grade D / ISO class 9 (dynamic) rooms buckets must be cleaned and dried before use. The mop heads, cloths and wipes should all be for single applications and should be discarded after use.

Cleaning and disinfection steps

The cleaning and disinfection process consists of:

- Sweeping away dust and debris (if applicable)

- Application of a detergent solution through wiping or mopping.
- Application of a disinfectant solution through wiping or mopping.
- Removal of disinfectant residue through wiping or mopping with Water for Injections or 70% IPA.

Areas to which a detergent is applied must be allowed to dry before the application of the disinfectant step.

During the cleaning process care should be taken not to damage any HEPA filters, especially by wetting them with cleaning agents. When a 'high level' clean is required, cleaning should commence with the ceiling followed by the walls and then floors. Benches, hatches, doors, cabinets and other cleanroom equipment should be cleaned by hand using low linting wipes. The detergent clean should be repeated until the bucket at the end of the process is free from solid particles and the mop head does not look dirty (9).

Disinfectants are only to be applied to areas that are clean and have had an appropriate detergent wash as applicable. This is because poorly cleaned areas or areas where there is a detergent residue could give some protection to microbial populations and impair disinfectant efficacy. Furthermore, disinfectants must not be used for cleaning purposes. Disinfectants for surfaces are only to be applied to clean areas, that is after the application of a detergent. This is undertaken through mopping and wiping, which allows the target location to be treated and the amount of disinfectant solution added to the surface to be controlled.

When a disinfectant has been applied the area must not be used until the contact time has elapsed. Different disinfectants have different contact times, based on manufacturer's recommendations, and these must be stated in local procedures. For the duration of the contact time, the disinfectant is to remain in contact with the surface. For floors, walls and ceilings this is 'visibly wet'. If drying out is noticed, additional applications must be performed.

After the application of a disinfectant it is normal practice to remove the residue. This is because residues, in theory, can lead to resistant microbial strains and often lead to discolouration or corrosion. Residues are removed using either WFI or IPA.

Cleaning techniques

The cleaning technique used for cleanrooms should be defined and standardised. It does not matter how effective the cleaning agents selected are if the cleaning technique practised by cleanroom operators is poor. This partly relates to the techniques used and partly to the quality of the cleaning materials, for improperly cleaned areas where organic matter remains or areas which have a detergent residue, could potentially confer some protection to microbial populations and impair the efficacy of the subsequently applied disinfectant. In many ways, the physical treatment of a surface or item of equipment is as important as the chemical.

Prior to the application of detergents, specialised equipment like dry vacuum cleaners (with HEPA filters), steam cleaners and floor scrubbing machines (where a volume of detergent is applied to the scrubbing pad) can be used for collection or removal of visible items of waste from floors. Wet vacuum machines can be used to remove water, spillages or even excess detergent residues. However, such devices can damage floors and act to disperse contamination across an area rather than remove it. It is important for such machines to be carefully cleaned and stored after use, and never to be left damp in order to avoid building up biocontamination.

Detergents and disinfectants for use on surfaces (walls, floors) must be applied using the double or triple-bucket system to avoid cross contamination. The triple-bucket system uses two buckets of disinfectant or detergent and one empty bucket (where the technique should be outlined in local procedures). Furthermore, appropriate records should be kept of cleaning activities in process areas.

Both of these techniques involve using a bucket of disinfectant and a bucket of water. In the "two-bucket" technique there is a "wringer" (for the mop) over the bucket of water. In the "three-bucket" technique there is a third bucket, empty except for having a wringer mounted over it. The two techniques involve preparing the detergent or disinfectant in front bucket according to instructions.

In terms of the materials used for cleaning, appropriate mops and wipes should be used. Wipes should be sterile and also low particle shedding. When using wipes for surfaces, the detergent or disinfectant should ideally be sprayed onto the surface rather than the wipe and left for the required contact time before wiping is undertaken (7). With mops, the mop head should be cleanroom compatible (such as a microfiber based yarn) and be single use. For Grade A and B areas, the mop heads should be sterile. Also of importance to such areas are the mops which should be autoclavable. The design of the mop is a further consideration and must be easy for the cleanroom operator to use and allow for a uniform application of the disinfectant solution.

It is important that disinfectant residues are removed to avoid the potential for microbial resistance. The final stage in floor cleaning and disinfection is typically a rinse with sterile Water for Injection. For Grade A / ISO class 5 and Grade B / ISO class 7 areas careful consideration is required as any water used needs to be sterile.

Cleaning and disinfection using cloths and mop heads is ideally performed by saturating the cleaning item and wiping the area using a series of parallel overlapping strokes (with an approximate one quarter overlap) and never in circular motions. The direction of the cleaning should be towards the operator (from top to bottom, from back to front). Only one application of the disinfectant or detergent should be applied to avoid over concentration. Cleaning and disinfection should begin with the visually 'cleanest' area first and towards the 'dirtiest' area last (typically the application of detergents or disinfectants involves starting from the far side of a room and towards the exit in a series of overlapping parallel strokes).

Cleaning and disinfection frequencies

Cleaning and disinfection sessions are performed at different frequencies for different areas. This is based on the criticality of the area and this will vary between facilities. The frequency is ideally established through risk assessment or based on empirical data, such as through a field trial (see below).

Cleaning and disinfection frequencies are often expanded through different parts of the cleanroom being cleaned or disinfected at different times ('levels of cleaning'). That is, floors and working surfaces will often be cleaned at a higher frequency than walls or ceilings.

8.8 Cleaning and disinfection protocols

Establishing a cleaning and disinfection protocol is an important step for a pharmaceutical organisation in its microbial control programme. An established and effective protocol will ensure that risks to the manufactured product or medical device are minimised. In drawing together a programme, advice is available from regulatory authorities (through cGMP) and consideration should be given to aspects discussed in this chapter: compatibility of detergents and disinfectants, the need for rotation, methods for cleaning and the results of method validation. Ideally the programme should be published within the organisation and it is important the staff are given sufficient time to carry out each cleaning step.

The procedures should cover the following aspects:

- The type of detergents and disinfectants to be used (which are compatible).
- The frequency of rotation of disinfectants.
- A list of suitable cleaning materials.
- Cleaning techniques.
- Contact times.
- Rinsing.
- Frequency of cleaning and disinfection.
- Procedure for the transfer of cleaning agents and disinfectants into and out of clean areas (including the procedure for sterilisation of disinfectants).
- Holding times for detergents and disinfectants (for how long, after preparation, can a detergent or disinfectant be used?).

When writing cleaning procedures it is good practice to involve the staff who will be undertaking the cleaning, so that the procedures are clear and easy to follow.

8.9 Assessing disinfectant effectiveness: environmental monitoring

To ensure the effectiveness of a cleaning and disinfection programme, microbiological environmental monitoring of surfaces and equipment is necessary. The primary methods for conducting these tests involve the use of cotton swabs (with a recovery diluent and later plating onto agar or dissolving prior to membrane filtration) and contact plates[6] or other surface agar techniques. The

[6] Contact plates are sometimes called RODAC (Replicate Organism Detection and Counting) plates

recovery efficiency of contact plates is generally superior to that of swab (10). The agars used should contain appropriate neutralising agents in order to eliminate any disinfectant residues and thus allow any recovered microorganisms to grow (this is discussed further in chapter ten). An appropriate general agar, such as soya-bean casein digest medium, is normally recommended. This agar, onto which swabs are sub-cultured or used in the contact plates, should have a dual incubation step designed to pick up a range of environmental microorganisms. A typical regimen would be 20–25°C for 48 hours followed by 30–35°C for 72 hours.

Figure 3: Laboratory technicians discussing the sampling of surfaces using contact plates (© Tim Sandle)

It is a regulatory requirement that the results of an environmental monitoring programme are examined at regular intervals for the development of resistant strains. How the pharmaceutical organisation reacts to the presence of a resistant strain varies, and the definition of a resistant strain (in terms of numbers, detection rate and spread of detection) will vary. The detection of a microorganism at a given location on successive occasions should not immediately lead to changing the disinfectant on a day-to-day basis. Some manufacturers argue that two disinfectants only need to be employed if the environmental monitoring data indicate excursions from set limits and therefore the one disinfectant is not controlling surfaces.

8.10 Validating disinfectants to be used in cleanrooms: field trials

Chapter Ten provides an overview of disinfectant validation. With the European approach to disinfectant validation, a third phase is recommended: field trials, although no official standard has yet been produced. Nonetheless, the concept of the field trial is an important one for it verifies that the cleaning and disinfection techniques and frequencies are suitable for the pharmaceutical operation. A field trial requires experimental planning.

Only disinfectants that have satisfactorily passed the previous phases should be studied for field trials. The purpose of field trials is to test a disinfectant's efficacy in practical in-use conditions: the working environment. Most researchers consider that a field trial is the only accurate test of a disinfectant, given the problems with repeatability and reproducibility associated with laboratory based tests. It is also because the trials examine a selected concentration on surfaces and equipment after the cleaning step has been applied. Field trials have an advantage because they test the disinfectant against a wide range of surfaces and with all the different types of interfering substances that may be present, as well as different physico-chemical conditions, like temperature and pH (11). The variable application of cleaning and disinfectant agents by different operators can also be considered. However, field trials can be costly to pharmaceutical companies both in terms of the cost of the study and the time taken to complete it.

Although no common European Standard exists, the common approach for field trials involves applying the disinfectant, at the selected concentration, to a selection of surfaces and equipment within the manufacturing facility. To these controlled areas, an intensive level of viable microbiological environmental monitoring is undertaken. Field trials are a test for both attached and suspended microorganisms, as well as allowing evaluation of a range of variables like cleaning technique; recovery of damaged cells; temperature; contact time; interfering substances and so on (12).

In conducting a trial the areas should be monitored prior to the introduction of the disinfectant and shown to be satisfactory against test criteria. (Normally the action levels for viable microorganisms on surfaces for a given cleanroom, such as, the recommended levels in the EU

GMP Guide). This would be performed by selecting a representative number of sites in a room and monitoring these locations using appropriate methods, such as swabs or contact plates, daily over a four week period. It would be prudent for the microbiologist to have evaluated any neutralisers in the culture media used for environmental monitoring against the disinfectants under test at this stage. Following the establishment of a baseline the new disinfectant would be applied to the test areas and the level of environmental monitoring sustained. The two sets of results would then be examined for any significant difference with the criteria being that the results after the application of the new disinfectant are equivalent to before or, ideally, better (that is fewer microorganisms recovered).

8.11 Summary

This chapter has, in the context of the pharmaceutical environment, examined the importance of the application of detergents and disinfectants within the pharmaceutical facility. The chapter has emphasised the importance of observing GMP and the consistent and careful use of such agents in accordance with SOPs.

There has been an emphasis in this chapter on the importance of a well-written policy to describe the agents which have been selected, and on a clear procedure, to describe the application of cleaning and disinfection agents. The precise content of such documents will depend upon the actual facilities and the requirements of national regulatory authorities.

The chapter has also touched upon other areas of regulatory expectation in relation to pharmaceutical processing, such as consideration for the need for sterile filtered solutions. In addition, good practice for field trials and the importance of the environmental monitoring programme have been discussed. As with other aspects of GMP, it is important to understand and to remain up-to-date with regulatory requirements.

8.12 References

1. Block, S. *Disinfection, Sterilisation and Preservation*, Third Edition, 1977, Philadelphia: Lea and Febiger
2. Sandle, T. (2014) Selection and use of Cleaning and Disinfection Agents in Pharmaceutical Manufacturing. In Handlon, G. and Sandle, T. (Eds.) *Industrial Pharmaceutical Microbiology: Standards & Controls*, Euromed Communications, Passfield, UK, 9.1–9.32
3. Euradlex. *The Rules Governing Medicinal Products in the European Community*, Annex 1, published by the European Commission, 2009.
4. ISO 14644-1: *Cleanrooms and associated controlled environments* - Part 1: Classification of air cleanliness. International Organization for Standardization ISO, Geneva (2015)
5. Anon. Bacteriotherapy: the time has come, British Medical Journal, 18th August 2001, 353–354.
6. Madigan M, Martinko J and Parker J. *Brock Biology of Microorganisms*, Eighth Edition, 1997, Prentice Hall, 408–409.
7. Baird, R. 'Cleaning and Disinfection in the hospital pharmacy' in Collins, C.H. (Ed.) *Disinfectants, their use and evaluation of effectiveness*. Society Applied Bacteriology TS16 p154 1981.
8. Sartain. E. K. 'Regulatory Update: Rotating Disinfectants in Cleanrooms: Avoid Going in Circles', *A2C2 Magazine*, Vol. 8, No. 3, March, 2005, pp. 32-33.
9. Cooper, D. (2000): 'Applying a Uniform Layer of Disinfectant by Wiping', *PDA Journal of*

Science and Technology, 2000, Vol.54, No. 1, pp44-58

10. Sandle, T. (2015) Contamination Control Risk Assessment. In McCullough, K.Z. and Moldenhauer, J. (Eds.) *Microbial Risks and Investigations*, DHI/PDA, River Grove, USA, pp783-836
11. Denny, V.F.; Marsik, F.J. Current Practices in the Use of Disinfectants within the Pharmaceutical Industry. *PDA J. of Pharmaceutical Sci. and Tech.*, 1997, Vol. 51, No.6, pp 227–228.
12. Holah, J.T., Lavaud, A., Peters, W. and Dye, K.A.: 'Future techniques for disinfectant efficacy testing', *International Biodeterioration and Biodegradation*, 41, 1998, pp273-279

CHAPTER 9:

GASEOUS DISINFECTION OF BARRIER SYSTEMS

By James Drinkwater and Laura Buck

9.1 Introduction

Controlled areas use a system of barriers to separate critical processes from surrounding contaminants (1) (Figure 1). In order to segregate these areas by EU GMP grade or ISO class, total particulate (particles of 0.5–5 microns, including everything from dust to skin cells) and all microorganisms must be controlled either by level or incidence rate; with Grade A/ ISO 5 having the most stringent requirements (2). Bio-contamination from people, including gowned operators, is known to be the most contaminating source (3). Barrier Separation technology such as Isolators (4) and Restricted Access Barrier Systems (RABS) (5) are used in a cleanroom environment to protect processes from contaminants. Separative barriers and their related zone-to-zone material transfer devices all require a disinfection program to control bio-burden and to meet classified conditions of microbiological control.

This chapter covers gaseous disinfection technology with a focus on the benchmark process – hydrogen peroxide (H_2O_2) vapour. Other disinfection processes including fumigation with formaldehyde and 'fogging' or aerosol distribution of H_2O_2 are compared. This chapter comprehensively reviews disinfection of controlled areas and does not cover other applications of gaseous decontamination such as decontamination of toxic components. It is hoped that this thorough overview will assist in selection of a disinfection technology and increase process knowledge.

The topics on gaseous disinfection of barriers covered in this chapter are:

- Overview of H_2O_2 vapour as the benchmark gaseous disinfection process
- Comparison of H_2O_2 vapour with other disinfection technologies
- Applications of gaseous disinfection in barrier systems
- The science of H_2O_2 vapour gaseous disinfection
- Hierarchy of Bio-decontamination and efficacy requirements and expectations in different zones
- Cycle development strategies using chemical and biological indicator challenge studies
- Critical Quality Attributes (CQAs) in control and monitoring of H_2O_2 vapour decontamination cycles
- Summary of the challenges and expectations

9.2 Overview of H_2O_2 vapour as the benchmark gaseous disinfection process

There are principle drivers as to why H_2O_2 vapour has been reported and widely cited as the benchmark

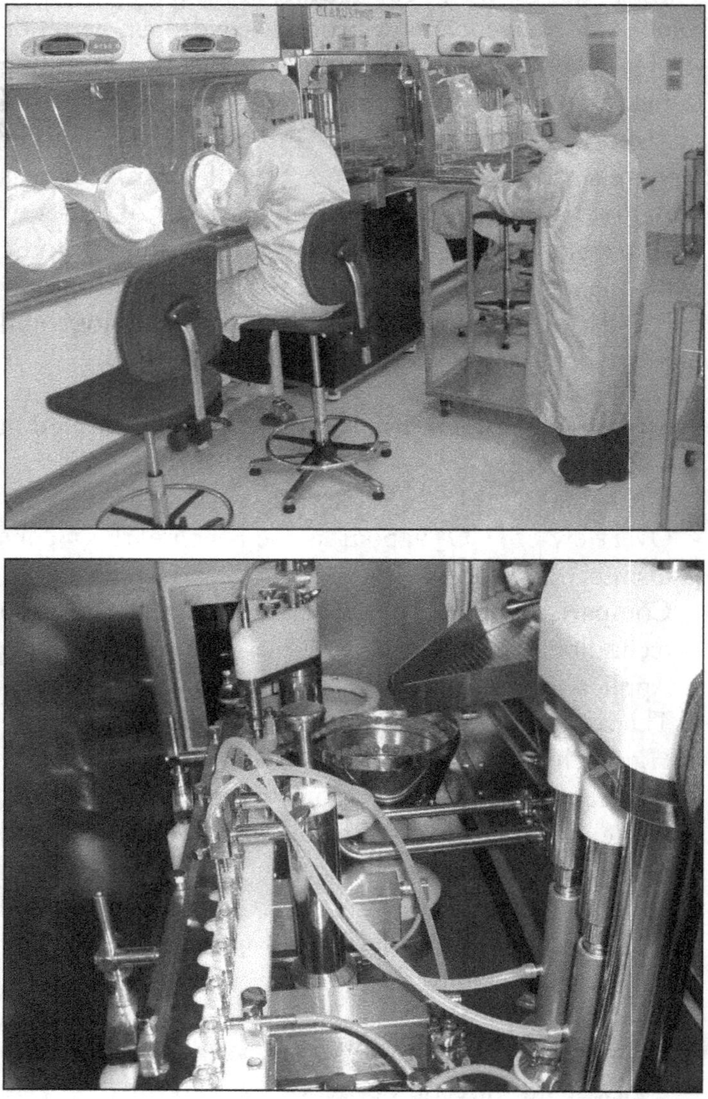

Figure 1. Pharmacy aseptic services Isolator and aseptic filling using closed design barriers.

gaseous disinfection process. The combination of broad spectrum efficacy and the low temperature and residue free process are fundamental to compatibility and performance for most disinfection processes (6, 7, 8). Following the sporicidal process, residual hydrogen peroxide is broken down to the innocuous components of oxygen and water both on contact with catalysts and in the environment on organic matter. In addition, the H_2O_2 vapour disinfection mode of action is well researched and increasingly well characterised. H_2O_2 vapour safety is fully manageable; with a typical 0.5-1 ppm operator exposure limit (OEL) time-weighted average over 8 hours.

Gaseous disinfection with H_2O_2vapour has numerous and increasing applications. In addition to its use in pharmaceutical and biopharmaceutical development and production facilities it is also used in: disinfection of process equipment such as freeze dryers, in food production (to increase shelf-life when cold chain distribution cannot be used), in the eradication of hospital acquired infections including certain nosocomial pathogens such as methicillin-resistant *Staphylococcus aureus* (MRSA), vancomycin-resistant *Enterococcus* (VRE), *Clostridium difficile, Acinetobacter* and other challenging viruses such as norovirus.

It should be understood from the outset that gaseous disinfection is a final step that requires a necessary pre-cleaning step. The target of the gaseous disinfection process is surface bio-decontamination and does not match the performance of defined penetrative sterilisation processes detailed in Pharmacopeia (9, 10). Although

H_2O_2 vapour has a little penetrative disinfection capability this is limited and difficult to validate. Surface gaseous disinfection requires a starting condition where a surface is visibly clean of soiling. Visible contamination or soiling may occlude microorganisms from the disinfection process and if uncovered in-process may present a bio-contamination risk.

A H_2O_2 decontamination process requires integration into any application with a special focus on system configuration, which must be suitable for vapour containment and exposure of all target surfaces together with delivery and removal of the decontaminating agent. In optimum gaseous disinfection processes, automation is used to configure any system for bio-decontamination plus to communicate with any associated H_2O_2 vapour generator such that the transitions between cycle phases are controlled without operator intervention. There are four key steps to the optimum H_2O_2 vapour disinfection process:

1. Vaporisation of liquid to small molecules – gas phase delivery to target volume.
2. Development of the gas concentration in the target environment to saturated vapour conditions, past dew point and transition into liquid phase.
3. Micro-condensation formation on surfaces by merging molecules. Initially nuclei form on any surface contaminants, before full condensation occurs over the entire available surface, eventually forming a disinfectant monolayer (from gas to liquid phase).
4. Re-evaporation of the surface condensate and removal of residual gas to target endpoint.

9.3 Comparison of H_2O_2 vapour with other disinfection technologies

Disinfection programs for Good Manufacturing Practice (GMP) require a sporicidal agent. Agents of marginal efficacy may need to be rotated, ideally different agents with different modes of action to overcome any building resistance or marginal efficacy. Manually applied sporicidal agents can be very aggressive to surfaces so are often rotated. Any sporicidal agent that is left wet on a surface without controlled removal will encourage and exacerbate corrosion or material damage.

Gaseous H_2O_2 vapour is a sporicidal agent of highly destructive microbial efficacy with controlled delivery, a short contact time with controlled removal and the process is residue free to facilitate compatibility, and thus rotation with other disinfection agents is not required.

It is understood that manual spray and wipe disinfection or use of impregnated wipes have a number of process variables, mainly relating to operator technique, which challenge the ability of the process to be validated. There are processes that use spray and wipe techniques to reduce bioburden but the process becomes challenged as a robust disinfection process when applied to critical zones or at critical material transfer disinfection steps, as some residual bio-contamination is likely (and variable). There are other critical factors that impact efficacy of manually applied disinfectants and these include the impact of filtered air from cleanroom ventilation drying the disinfection agent such that the contact time is cut short with a resulting reduction in efficacy.

In contrast, gaseous disinfection processes are automated, have parameters of control that can be monitored and alarmed in deviation. To achieve effective bio-decontamination the barrier system must be isolated from ventilation such that bio-decontamination conditions of process lethality (determined for any defined process as appropriate) can be developed without dilution effects. Gaseous surface disinfection processes are validated with biological indicator (BI) challenges that are typically highly resistant to the agent used, and much more resistant than flora naturally occurring in the controlled area (11).

Gaseous vapour phase disinfection technologies are typically referred to as 'Wet' or 'Dry' vapour processes. Wet processes are those that operate past dew point in saturated vapour conditions such that micro-condensation forms. Dry processes are those that stay short of dew point relying on distribution of vaporised molecules and dynamic contact with surfaces (see 9.5 The science of H_2O_2 vapour gaseous disinfection for further detail).

If the process only extends to the gas phase, staying short of dew point and saturated vapour, it is concluded that molecules only make random contact with surfaces hence this is not an efficient targeted process of agent delivery. In this gas phase efficacy will still be achieved but the inactivation process is likely to be more variable in complex areas with multiple surfaces leading to longer disinfection cycles.

The alternative to vapour distribution are atomised 'foggers' primarily as disinfectant delivery systems, which are an improvement on manual disinfectant application, but like manual disinfection have no controlled residual removal. Foggers can have safety implications with background levels above the 1 ppm OEL (circa 2 ppm) remaining for some considerable time as surface disinfectants continue to evaporate into the environment .

A further consideration when comparing vaporisation versus atomisation (in foggers) is molecule size. In the gas phase before molecules merge the vaporized molecule size is in the pico range (10^{-12}). In comparison atomized molecule sizes from a fogger or nebuliser are within the micron range. As a relative physical comparison, if you consider the vapour molecule as the size of a golf ball then atomized molecules would be the size of the Empire State building. Such a variance has an impact on gas distribution and access to bio-contamination.

Disinfection 'foggers' have found challenges with BI kill (12), hence limiting the application. In fogger BI challenge studies, due mainly to issues of the atomised molecule size passing through the Tyvek pouch, the BI pouches often have to be open to expose the BI inoculums or the BI has to be so wetted that eventually H_2O_2 permeates through the Tyvek to make contact with the inoculated disc.

Atomised fogger systems tend to let molecules settle, relying on Brownian motion for distribution rather than saturated vapour conditions, and the surface process is more 'static', as with spray-on disinfectants. This results in less effective bio-decontamination as any breakdown of H_2O_2 due to initial catalytic effects, catalase positive micro-organisms etc, is not replenished as it would be in a dynamic gaseous vapour disinfection. Foggers do have a place in general disinfection but cannot be truly compared to gaseous disinfection.

There are other gaseous disinfection processes that have the high levels of efficacy comparable with H_2O_2 vapour e.g. chlorine dioxide gas and peracetic acid. Such processes have additional safety issues due to highly diffusive gas containment, with much lower operator exposure limits e.g. 0.1 ppm in the case of chlorine dioxide, and furthermore reported material compatibility issues have resulted in limitations of application.

Traditionally fumigation of cleanrooms and some Isolators were (and in some cases still are) completed with a formaldehyde fumigant. When the World Health Organisation (WHO) reclassified formaldehyde as carcinogenic (13), this brought about a step change in cleanroom gaseous disinfection with a move towards H_2O_2 vapour disinfection. H_2O_2 vapour is a safer and more convenient alternative due to the residue free process and thanks to the hydrogen bonding characteristics of H_2O_2. This bonding property means that the vapour is poor at passive diffusion and reduces risks to operators since leaks will 'hang' in the locality and not spread. This facilitates decontamination of rooms with occupants in adjacent areas. In contrast local leaks of a highly diffusive gas such as formaldehyde would spread around a facility and present a risk of extensive personnel exposure. Adjacent areas are usually evacuated to avoid risk of exposure to formaldehyde gas.

9.4 The application of gaseous disinfection in barrier systems

Gaseous disinfection of barrier systems can refer to cleanrooms, Isolators and RABS as well as material transfer chambers or ports, and the supporting process zones. The diagram in Figure 2 demonstrates how these barriers may interact.

Typically Barrier separation technology is used for critical areas which are EU Grade A/ ISO 5 (i.e. the more contained separation barrier technology; Isolators and RABS). These critical areas and the supporting process zones benefit from the higher level of efficacy, repeatability, automation in control and monitoring afforded by H_2O_2 vapour processes. Risks are managed by controlling critical parameters in the process with deviations monitored and alarmed.

Isolators have had a history of gaseous disinfection with H_2O_2 vapour and recently (2010) the development of closed RABS has also facilitated use of the gaseous disinfection process and gassing-in-place (GIP) of indirect product contact parts such as feeder bowls and stopper track-ways.

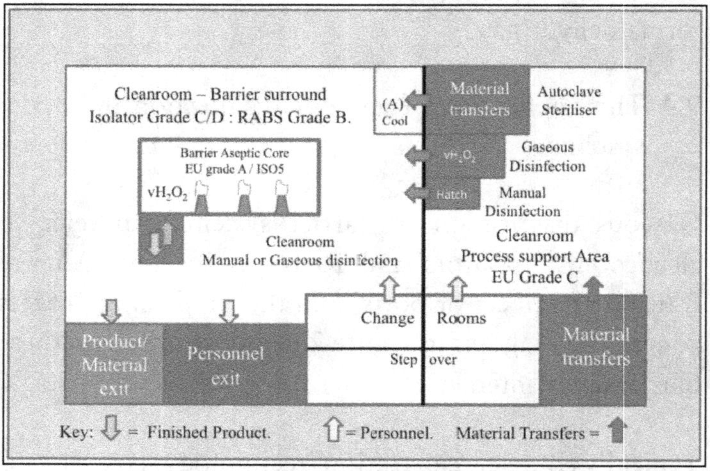

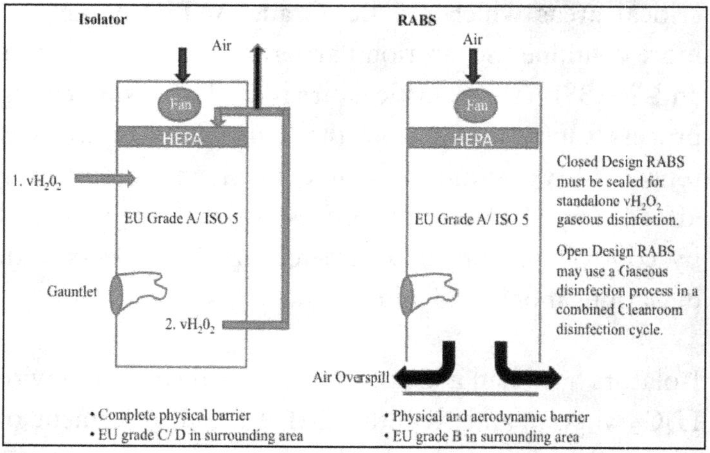

Figure 2A) Barrier systems
Figure 2B) barrier separation technology

In barrier systems to control bio-contamination the following measures are taken:

- At entry to cleanrooms, personnel change into special sterile gowning to control bio-contamination ingress to facilities.
- Direct product contact parts are either cleaned or sterilised in place (CIP/SIP) or a sterilisation step completed out of place with transfer to the process and aseptic assembly.
- Indirect product contact parts may be sterilised out of place, followed by cool down, transfer and aseptically assembled in the Separation barrier (Isolator or RABS) or Gassed in place (GIP).
- Consumable parts or wrapped sterile parts part may have the outer surface of the sterile packaging disinfected at a barrier transfer by manual procedures (in a transfer hatch) or by gaseous disinfection (in a Material gassing transfer chamber or Port).
- Non-contact parts and supporting facilities may use a manual or gaseous disinfection or less stringent sanitisation process.

Today, with the increase of products with a biological profile, in particular virus-based products, there is an additional need for environmental virus clearance between product campaigns and to prevent cross-contamination of biological products between controlled areas. H_2O_2 vapour disinfection offers that option and is now considered for biological facilities. Processes are validated with BI challenges and typically both sporicidal and virus inactivation studies are completed to characterise process efficacy. However, there are some disinfection compatibility challenges with biological products that are protein based or impacted by the oxidising potential of H_2O_2 vapour. In these cases cycle endpoint studies have a focus on ensuring residual oxidising impact is extremely low – at parts per billion (ppb) level and not just a focus on operator safety (at ppm level).

Increasingly it is recognised that manual disinfection of material surfaces at zone-to-zone transfer steps may result in variable bioburden entering a controlled area. Gaseous disinfection transfer chambers and rapid gassing ports have been developed to meet the aim of more efficacy and repeatability of disinfection. Such transfer devices need optimum and fast cycle times if they are to be on the critical path of a process flow. The development of rapid gassing technology has facilitated just in time delivery of required materials to processes so decontaminated batches of materials/supplies can be transferred to critical areas with total cycle times within the region of 15–20 minutes.

As gaseous disinfection processes are developed with robust and easy to use bio-decontamination cycles then, like Isolators, even within cleanrooms the process may become the norm replacing labour intensive manual disinfection. In this case manual processes would simply be used for pre-cleaning; removing visible soiling that in turn would reduce bioburden ahead of disinfection.

9.5 The science of H_2O_2 vapour gaseous disinfection

H_2O_2 vapour is a USA Environmental Protection Agency (EPA) registered vapour-phase sterilant and is well established as a bio-decontamination agent due to its broad-spectrum efficacy and its ability to rapidly inactivate the most resilient micro-organisms. H_2O_2 vapour has proven biological efficacy against a wide range of micro-organisms including bacterial endospores (14), mycobacteria (15), vegetative bacteria (16), atypical bacteria (17), viruses (18) and fungi (19). Typically the decontaminating vapour is generated by flash evaporation from 30% (wt/wt) liquid H_2O_2.

The H_2O_2 vapour disinfection process employs a free radical reaction mechanism to facilitate microbiocidal action. Free radicals are highly energetic atoms or molecules that possess an unpaired electron (Figure 3).

The unpaired electron is compelled to exist in a paired state and will physically strip an electron from another

Figure 3. Free radicals possess an unpaired electron

compound to promote pairing. This ability makes these compounds extremely effective against microbiological organisms, since there is no target site specificity it makes it very difficult to develop resistance to free radical attack.

H_2O_2 vapour can, on exposure to a range of compounds including organic matter, give rise to the formation of the highly reactive hydroxyl (OH·) radical (20) (Figure 4). OH· is one of the strongest oxidants known having a very high oxidization potential and low specificity resulting in the broad spectrum efficacy (Table 1).

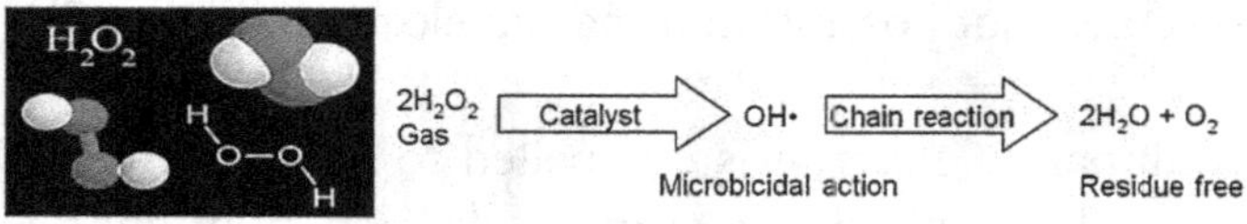

Figure 4. H2O2 is a powerful oxidising agent; it is converted to a highly reactive free radical. The end products of the chain reaction are harmless oxygen and water.

Oxidizing Reagent/Oxidizing Potential	
Flourine	3.06
Hydroxyl radicals	2.80
Atomic oxygen	2.42
Ozone	2.07
Hydrogen peroxide	1.77
Chlorine dioxide	1.50
Hypochlorus acid (HOCl)	1.49

Table 1. The oxidizing potential of each chemical refers to its ability to strip electrons from a material.

9.5.1 H_2O_2 targets and action in the bacterial cell

The hydroxyl (OH·) radical can attack essential cell components causing cell death. It is believed to be the principle mechanism by which H_2O_2 kills bacteria (21). Oxidative biocides such as H_2O_2 are proposed to have multiple targets within a cell; being destructive to cell envelopes, causing intracellular damage and cleaving DNA. The hydroxyl radical removes electrons from susceptible chemical groups, oxidizing them and is itself reduced in the process (22). Mechanisms of biological inactivation include peroxidation and disruption of membrane layers, oxidation of oxygen scavengers and thiol groups, inhibition of metabolic processes (notably protein synthesis), oxidation and breakage of nucleosides, impaired energy production and damage to cytoplasmic structures (21, 23, 24, 25, 26, 27). These processes can damage virtually all types of macromolecules including carbohydrates, nucleic acids, lipids and proteins. In addition, in the presence of myeloperoxide enzyme (MPO), chlorine in bacteria may be oxidized by H_2O_2 to hypochlorite (OCl·). The latter is a well-known oxidant and germicide possessing antimicrobial action (21, 28).

9.5.2 H_2O_2 vapour distribution and delivery mechanisms

Vaporised H_2O_2 molecules have to make contact with surfaces to affect bio-decontamination by the free radical attack process. The mechanism of molecule distribution and gas-to-liquid phase change is well characterised and understood (29). Micro-condensation formation is a simple and efficient way of delivering the agent to all exposed surfaces (Figure 5). The poor passive diffusion of H_2O_2 vapour is a redeeming factor for safety but challenging for delivery. In process it is therefore essential to distribute molecules via kinetic energy using distribution jet nozzles or fan ventilators.

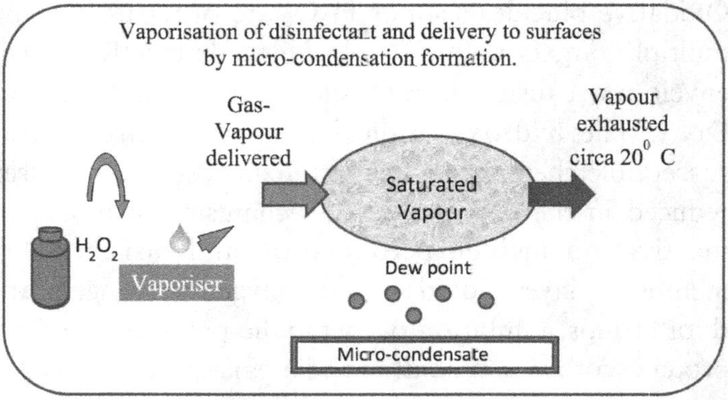

Figure 5. The disinfectant delivery mechanism to target surfaces by micro-condensation formation.

Recent research from a team based in Germany found that more than a few microns of molecule-monolayer deposition (which is invisible micro-condensation) contributes nothing additional to the efficacy of the process (30). So really optimum bio-decontamination processes are between the 'Wet' visible condensation condition (with over injection of vapour) and the invisible gas phase –'Dry' process that is specified to stay short of dew point. This research has put an end to the debate of which is the best gaseous disinfection process, the so-called 'Wet versus Dry debate', as the science defines that optimum kill conditions are neither 'Wet or Dry' and requires dew point to be reached. Achieving dew point in a target volume of gas is impacted by starting temperature, relative humidity conditions and the subsequent amount of vapour injected into the target volume.

To understand why there is no real additional efficacy with visible condensation you have to consider the dynamic state of the process. In equilibrium there are as many molecules arriving on the surface as leaving- a dynamic state. Molecules in contact with surfaces have the reactive effect and are reduced; with continued surface exchange, efficacy is maintained. Consider if the surface condensate was visible but like a deep sea there would be upper surface exchange with very little impact on the sea bed (target surface to bio-decontaminate).

In practical applications at saturated vapour conditions there may be slight misting, due to the thermal differential across a screen/window between the target area and surround. If viewed inside the Isolator/ cleanroom there should be no visible condensation on any other surface (otherwise this is just poor cycle development or process configuration – something that happened in the past).

9.6 Hierarchy of bio-decontamination and efficacy requirements and expectations in different zones

There is a hierarchy of bio-decontamination processes with sterilisation being the highest level, as a fully penetrative process. All other processes (gaseous or manual disinfection and sanitisation) are surface treatment processes (Table 2).

Bio-Decontamination process	Efficacy validation	Principle method(s)	Target surfaces	Cleaning requirement	Residue management
1. Sterilisation	Challenged with BIs for $6_{\log 10}$ sporicidal efficacy.	Moist heat, dry heat, Gamma irradiation, Ethylene oxide (ETO)	Direct product contact parts.	Reduction and characterisation of starting bioburden	Only applies to ETO as a gas residual.
2. Gaseous Vapour Phase (GVP) decontamination	Challenged with BIs for $6_{\log10}$ sporicidal efficacy.	H_2O_2 Vaporisation by flash evaporation.	Gassing in place (GIP) for indirect product contact parts.	Chemical cleaning agents should be validated as residue free so that they do not compound with H_2O_2	Decontamination process requires validation as residue free to avoid chemical contamination of products.
3. Gaseous Disinfection	Challenged with BIs for target efficacy $3_{\log10}$ to $6_{\log10}$ sporicidal efficacy.	Vaporisation by flash evaporation of disinfection / sterilant agent	Material transfer chamber or Barriers: cleanrooms, Isolators, RABS.	Cleaning endpoint to be visibly clean (soiling would prevent occlusion of disinfection).	Disinfection cycle endpoint to be validated to reach target ppm level.

4. Fogging Disinfection	Challenged with BIs for target efficacy typically $3_{\log10}$ to $4_{\log10}$ sporicidal efficacy.	Atomised disinfectant delivered via pressurisation through nozzle(s).	Cleanrooms and RABS barriers.	Cleaning endpoint to be visibly clean (soiling would prevent occlusion of disinfection).	Not controlled - relies on evaporation and agent biodegradation.
5. Manual Disinfection	Challenged on inoculated surfaces with target efficacy on isolates typically $3_{\log10}$ to $4_{\log 10}$ sporicidal efficacy.	Disinfectants manually applied via mop and bucket or impregnated wipes.	Cleanrooms, Material surfaces in transfer and RABS/Isolator barriers.	Pre-cleaning requires visibly clean endpoint. Disinfection and cleaning may be combined e.g. spray and wipe or impregnated wipes. Any detergents used will require a residue removal step before disinfection.	Not controlled relies on evaporation and agent biodegradation.
6. Sanitisation	Uses laboratory validated agents (suspension tests) but not challenged with BIs. Environment monitored to review impact of sanitisation on bio-contamination control.	Disinfectants manually applied via mop and bucket or impregnated wipes.	Process support cleanrooms.	Typically a combined cleaning and bioburden reduction process using mop-applied sanitisation agents and rinses with multiple buckets.	Not controlled relies on evaporation and agent biodegradation.

Table 2. Hierarchy of bio-decontamination

H_2O_2 vapour gaseous disinfection processes are typically validated for efficacy with BI challenges known to be highly resistant to the agent and of higher resistance than bioburden that is found (normally resident or transient) in the target area for disinfection.

Disinfection sporicidal reduction is measured by log reduction (Table 3). One log reduction is 90% reduction in spore population, or a division of population by ten. For example, if one starts with one million spores then six steps of reduction (6_{log10}) would result in a population of one, which is one million divided by ten six times. Overkill conditions can be applied to the cycle for security i.e. > 6_{log10} reduction in spores.

Critical area	Sporicidal reduction (minimum)	Efficacy Validation by Spore BI required?
EU Grade A/ ISO 5	6_{log10}	Yes
EU Grade B / ISO 7 surrounding Grade A/ ISO5	$4_{log\ 10}$	Yes
EU Grade C/ ISO 8	3_{log10}	Optional
EU Grade D/ ISO n/a	3_{log10}	Optional

Table 3. Disinfection requirements for critical areas

Research has previously focused on kill efficiency and distribution mechanisms, but with the new range of biological products impacted by oxidizing agents, processes that control removal (rather than just wait for uncontrolled bio-degradation) have come into focus. Consequently there have been new developments in analytical technologies to study H_2O_2 endpoints, permeability and potential bio-product contamination. Gas concentrations can be measured (using laser technology) down to parts per billion (ppb) levels. H_2O_2 residual presence in solutions can also be studied at ppb levels using co-enzyme florescence based detection technology (31).

Catalyst technology (now very efficient) is part of the vapour generator system to control residual removal. H_2O_2 will not exist on stainless steel as it is a mild catalyst, but can compound with other chemical (cleaning) agent residuals, so if there are risks of mechanical transfer of residuals to a product then studies are required. Such studies (and potential residuals) are increasingly significant in biotechnology.

Where environmental viral clearance is required then a high level of sporicidal efficacy is typically applied e.g. $6_{\log 10}$ sporicidal reduction and possibly additional overkill if correlation studies demonstrate virus inactivation is more resistant to the process. It is difficult to complete viral inactivation studies as a routine and often spore form BIs are used as a proxy, with inactivation correlation between spores and viruses.

9.7 Cycle development strategies using chemical and biological indicator challenge studies

Characterisation studies are required to develop gaseous disinfection cycles, including both collective and iterative studies. Together these studies yield information on process variables and the transition between sub-lethal to lethal efficacies (using biological indicator challenges). *Geobacillus stearothermophilus* spore form biological indicators are the recognised standard for H_2O_2 vapour (11). BIs consist of dried-on spore inoculums on a stainless steel carrier and contained in a Tyvek primary pack (Figure 6). A positive or negative kill result is achieved, tested for by inoculating growth media with the BIs exposed to the disinfection cycle.

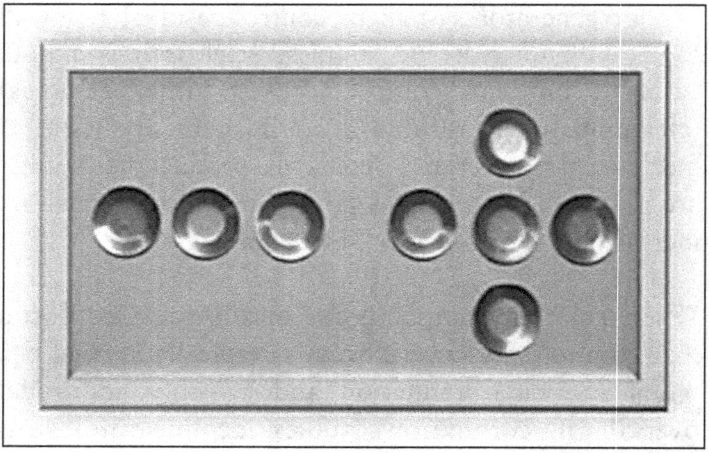

Figure 6. Stainless steel carriers typically used for biological indicators, Tyvek primary pouch not shown.

BIs are used in validation studies and not routinely to monitor disinfection cycle efficacy. Compared to the accurate monitoring of controlled disinfection cycle parameters, environmental monitoring has limitations; for example, poor recovery during sampling and analysis. Nonetheless, this is the best technology currently available and the only way to check if bio-contamination control is maintained in the environment and on specified surfaces after a bio-decontamination process and in process operations.

Common causes of process inefficiency include:

- **Delivery losses** – H_2O_2 vapour is evaporated by flash evaporation and is a condensable vapour, not a true gas. Delivery losses are therefore common due to reduction in the temperature of the high concentration vapour stream resulting in condensation before the vapour reaches target areas.
- **Delivery route** – Some surfaces are highly absorbent, including high efficiency particulate air (HEPA) filter media, and this needs to be considered in cycle development, and ideally avoided as the primary vapour delivery route to target areas.
- **Dry conditions** – As reaching dew point is critical then there is little point dehumidifying the environment to reach a very low level of humidity before vapour injection. Studies confirm that even at starting conditions of 75%RH there is more than enough efficacy at saturated vapour conditions via the surface micro-condensate. A more optimum 50%RH starting condition may be considered suitable for most applications.

Disinfection cycle characterisation

Characterisation of the temperatures inside the target area before starting and during the gaseous disinfection bio-decontamination process is essential because of the potential impact on efficacy. A study of starting temperatures on surfaces (following routine production use and before starting the disinfection cycle) will verify the process variable of temperature and influence from the equipment or surround. Analysis throughout the bio-decontamination process will give an overview of the impact and distribution of the relatively hot incoming disinfection vapour.

Gas concentration profiles carried out should be studied as part of cycle development and such profiles, compared cycle to cycle, indicate repeatability of the decontamination process and that the process is under control and not impacted further by variables. The cycle parameters of peroxide injection rates and phase times are initially developed to ascertain the required gas concentration profile. The optimum is a rapid rise to plateau conditions followed by near plateau conditions.

Having studied gas-vapour delivery and concentration profiles the next iterative study is gas distribution by use of chemical indicators (CIs). By placing colour change or 'water bag' chemical indicators around different challenging locations the rate and local concentration development can be studied.

Colour change indicators should be compared from first to last in time taken to change colour, indicating different rates of vapour concentration development. CI or vapour generator manufacturers can provide a time span expectation but typically for optimum cycles a span <5 minutes in the first to last colour change would be likely (but this is only guidance and is CI dependent).

Where CIs and resulting colour change cannot be seen from the observation area the typical approach is to place small, thin (2 ml) polythene bags of water in challenging locations. The thin wall of the bag permits H_2O_2 to permeate and pass into the water, which has an affinity for H_2O_2, and will hold and retain the sample. After the cycle a colour-change dipstick indicator can be placed in the water-peroxide sample and different colour gradients indicate how effective gas distribution was.

Once cycle parameters are developed that yield saturated vapour conditions and demonstrate acceptable gas distribution, then efficacy challenge studies can begin with BIs.

Typically BIs have *Geobacillus stearothermophilus* spore inoculations of an approximate population of 2 million, so that even with only 50% recovery of spores during verification, the resulting inactivation (kill) studies can prove 6_{log10} efficacy e.g. from 1 million to 1 spore in six log steps and with a little overkill, full inactivation.

It is essential that pre-use system D-value studies are completed on BIs to control for potential poor quality BIs that would impact validation studies and not be a suitable reference in studies of process variability. Such poor quality BIs are a result of poor manufacture and uncontrolled contamination in the inocula, leading to significant resistance variability and would be a poor indicator of cycle efficacy and control repeatability.

Following a review of BI location placement, selected for critical and worst case locations, BI challenge studies can then be completed and recorded on a 'BI map'.

Initially an expected overkill cycle is used to confirm 100% BI inactivation together with a rationale to manage any potential "Rogue BI's" (32). Rogues are highly resistant and out of trend (in a batch lot) BIs and expected in low numbers e.g. 1 in 300.

Following the full inactivation BI studies then further studies should reduce or optimise cycle parameters (injection rates or times) to transition from full kill into the fractional field where BIs partly survive –showing turbid growth in a suitable growth media, such as tryptone soya broth (TSB).

With the final BI kill studies completed then studies can advance to aeration endpoints; the time to remove residuals (micro-condensate and gaseous vapour) down to the target endpoint which is routinely set to 0.5-1 ppm (safe OEL). However, endpoints may differ based on process requirements. Lower target concentrations in cycle endpoints may be set if products to be processed are biological and affected by the oxidising potential of even very low concentrations of H_2O_2.

By combing the iterative study data the to characterise the cycle, parameters of control can be set and validated for routine use.

Re-qualification cycles are monitoring cycles that verify continued cycle efficacy and repeatable performance. Re-qualification studies are typically carried out annually and follow trended routine environmental monitoring data, so there can be a reduction (from that of validation) in the amount of cycles with BI challenges and a possible reduction in BI challenge locations (providing that critical areas are still studied and monitoring trends are as expected).

9.8 Critical Quality Attributes (CQAs) in control and monitoring of H_2O_2 vapour decontamination cycles

The importance of integrating the disinfection process into a specified production or research process should not be underestimated and failure to complete or execute the correct project stage may lead to long inefficient cycles even if biological challenge efficacy is proven. Key elements for regulatory acceptance of a gaseous disinfection process are that the science is understood behind the process and that there is a clear understanding of critical control points on which to base a system of control, monitoring and alarm. This section explains the optimum disinfection process (using micro-condensation), the science supporting the critical control points together with consideration of process variables, their control and monitoring. The parameters of control include: pressure, flow, injection rate, temperature and relative humidity. These parameters are collectively monitored on individual instruments and any one that deviates results in a critical alarm (cycle aborted).

Condensation formation at saturated vapour conditions, past dew point, as a mechanism to deliver the H_2O_2 molecules to all exposed surfaces is physical chemistry and hence has physical parameters of control. Presentation of surfaces to the disinfection process is extremely important. Material loads often rely on point contact support, via wire racking or hangers, to assure exposure to the disinfection agent.

At equilibrium saturated vapour conditions (during the micro-condensation process) there are six orders of magnitude more hydrogen molecules on the surface than at conditions before dew point (Dry process); hence the process conditions are optimum for secure and rapid sporicidal disinfection. H_2O_2 molecules that exist in the gas volume, measured as parts per million (ppm), have a direct relationship with micro-condensation (and disinfection) on target surfaces.

At saturated vapour conditions the gas concentration can hold no more molecules hence the process of condensation formation and disinfection agent surface deposition starts. This saturated condition is represented by a 'plateau' in environment gas concentration. Gas concentration profiles (Figure 7), are therefore important cycle characterisation studies and cycle-to-cycle comparisons typically indicate if the process is under control or subject to significant process variability.

Having scientific evidence that optimum efficacy in achieving biological inactivation is when the condition of micro-condensation is met means that the emphasis in process control is the rapid achievement of lethal conditions (and holding the conditions to accommodate process variables) and of repeatable and automated process control that can be validated.

The prevention of over-delivery of the agent to avoid excessive condensation is important, as without increased

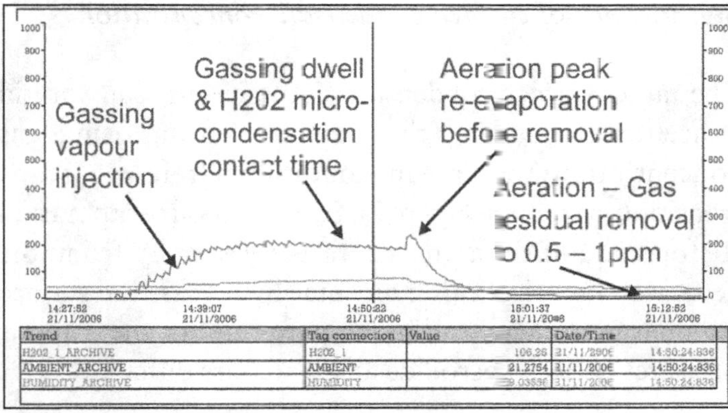

Figure 7. Gas concentration profile

efficacy the only real impacts are an increase in total cycle time to remove unnecessary residuals and increased potential for material damage. These essential requirements for optimum control are all parameters that can be studied, controlled, monitored and alarmed providing a robust process.

Primary process variables using H_2O_2 vapour include:

- Starting relative humidity (RH)
- Surface and environmental temperatures
- Gas distribution for a homogeneous deposition of vapour and resulting surface condensate.
- The amount of evaporated H_2O_2 solution dosed into the target volume (g/min) to reach saturated vapour conditions and provide a sufficient monolayer of disinfectant
- Surface area for condensate distribution together with amount of surface absorbency (e.g. packaging).

Significance of surface condensate concentration

The target surface condensate (2-6 microns) can vary in concentration during the transition from rising gas concentration to plateau conditions (referred to as transition events, see Figure 7). Forced vapour evaporation (before equilibrium in the target volume) from the generator vaporiser can momentarily increase the surface condensate concentration of peroxide as the vapour pressures between peroxide and water are different.

These transition events benefit efficacy for small volumes and lead to more rapid cycles where the ramp in gas concentration is rapid. In larger room volumes there is a smoother transition to equilibrium so peroxide concentrations in the condensate remain around 30%/ 35% w/w (that of the starting agent).

Significance of gas concentration in the enclosed environment – gas volume

H_2O_2 gas concentration (ppm) in the enclosed volume cannot be used directly (at fixed levels) for process control due to the current limitations of gas sensor technology and inherent process variables.

Sensors that see high concentrations are subject to slow recovery, cell degradation and a calibration accuracy of ± 5%. New gas sensor technology is in development, but currently electrochemical cells are used.

Gas concentration will vary cycle to cycle through natural changes in starting relative humidity and temperature. Such trends need review so that alert levels, used for monitoring can take account of such inherent deviation in ppm levels. Deviations in ppm levels do not mean ineffective cycles, as this only relates to the gas volume and what is occurring (micro-condensation) on the surface is the important condition for disinfection.

For 'alert level' ppm monitoring a H_2O_2 gas sensor is used with direct monitoring in the critical environment, monitoring through the complete decontamination process, and data recorded at cycle phase transitions.

The significance of starting relative humidity

When considering room volumes the difference in time to reach micro-condensation conditions is a lot higher for a large room than for that of a small chamber/ Isolator (Table 3), so cycle development has to consider 'worst case' and ensure injection overkill accommodates the time to reach worst case from the real-time study results.

Worst case conditions are the lowest starting %RH and the highest starting temperatures (both in the environment and on target surfaces).

Significance of temperature in the process

In small volumes, such as Isolators and Material transfer chambers (small in comparison to rooms), the temperature and relative humidity have very little impact on achieving condensation conditions, provided direct vapour injection systems are used which rapidly achieve

Volume of enclosure, room or room suite	Vapour generator parameters – H_2O_2 max injection rate 8 grams per minute, flow rate 30 cubic metre/hr and delivery temp 50°C	At starting temp of 22°C and %RH of worst case 20%RH (example 1). Time to reach starting condensation conditions and grams injected	At starting temp of 22°C and %RH at high 70%RH (example 2). Time to reach starting condensation conditions and grams injected
cubic metre	4 grams/min in gassing. 2 g/min in gassing dwell.	1 minute with 3.8 grams injected.	Less than 1 minute with 0.9 grams injected.
(10) cubic metres	8 g/min in gassing. 8 g/min in gassing dwell.	5 minutes with 39 grams injected.	1 minute with 9 grams injected.
(100) cubic metres	8 g/min in gassing. 8 g/min in gassing dwell.	48 minutes with 382 grams injected.	I2 minutes with 94 grams injected.
(350) cubic metres	8 g/min in gassing. 8 g/min in gassing dwell.	I67 minutes with 1339 grams injected.	41 minute with 329 grams injected.

Table 3. Effect on time to reach starting micro-condensation conditions as a result of variation in starting condition of RH% (humidity) at a typical starting temperature (environment)

the desired conditions with minimum delivery loss. In such small volumes (around one cubic metre) within the temperature range of 15–35°C and 15-75%RH the impact in time to reach condensation conditions is less than one minute, a time typically far less than the overkill cycle time added for security.

Higher initial starting temperatures mean that it takes longer to reach condensation conditions on surfaces. The reduction of temperature variability impacts the development rate of surface condensation. If there is a wide variance in surface temperatures then there will be variance in the rate of formation of condensate, hence variation in contact time, location to location. To optimise processes the temperature variation should be minimised, typically <5°C from hottest to coolest position.

When gaseous disinfection cycles start the vaporiser needs pre-heating ready for flash evaporation. For reference H_2O_2 is vaporized at 105°C. Hot vapour – typically delivered at 60°C – needs to be distributed so that surfaces are not heated locally above ~30°C to ensure an efficient process in validation. Care should be taken not to overheat BIs as the thin substrate takes on heat very quickly unlike target surfaces.

There is an important temperature interaction between hot surfaces from a previous sterilisation process and requirements for disinfection that must be considered in cycle development.

Investigations as a result of breech in the gas concentration alert level

Gas concentration alert levels are used to monitor gaseous disinfection cycles in routine use. Although such ppm levels have inherent variability; by trending, a minimum ppm reading in the gassing phase can be set, and if compromised this indicates atypical deviations.

From industry the following model has been developed for setting the ppm alert level.

Over a series of 10 cycles from the gassing phase of the cycle a standard deviation in ppm is calculated. Double the standard deviation is used to set a low alert level ppm value, subtracted from the mean ppm value monitored in the 10 cycle series. A lower alert level is used at a specific cycle phase. No upper ppm level is set.

Breach of the alert level should promote an investigation to confirm a valid disinfectant was used, the correct cycle was used and that it was alarm free. Deviations in ppm levels may also be the result of gas sensor calibration drift.

Optimisation of every process stage for rapid cycle times. Process stages:

Gaseous disinfection processes typically include four phases of control:

1. Conditioning – Initial temperature and relative humidity conditioning, before vapour injection. Hot dry air is first exchanged with the target environment to achieve required starting humidity conditions.

2. Gassing – Gassing may be optimised by use of direct injection to rapidly achieve process lethal conditions. By use of gas distribution nozzles and/or fan ventilators then the potential to produce hot spots from the incoming hot gas is controlled. With high velocity gas jets and gas/vapour expansion from the nozzle the vapour soon cools, with very effective and rapid mixing for fast formation of micro-condensation conditions.

The gassing phase is validated to deliver a disinfection agent dose volume that will reach required micro-condensation conditions in the target area and on target surfaces. Reaching such optimum conditions will be slowed down by injection and delivery of vapour via absorbent HEPA filters in the Barrier system. HEPA filters do have to be disinfected in the barrier system, but by directly injecting to process lethal conditions then circulating through air return paths and HEPA filters the cycle can be optimised in time and amount of H_2O_2 used. The 'alert level' check would be applied in this phase.

3. Gassing dwell /decontamination phase (contact time) – Dwell is optimised to maintain micro-condensation conditions throughout the complete dwell phase for assured disinfectant contact time. Gassing dwell is typically a process logic controller (PLC) time controlled phase. Cycle overkill (to accommodate process variables) is studied, and inherent process variability is added to the dwell time in gassing cycle development.

4. Aeration – Gas residual removal is typically achieved with integral or supporting HEPA-catalysts and/or supporting dilution via barrier air being vented to the environment.

Rationale for setting cycle overkill to achieve greater than $6_{\log 10}$ reduction.

Studies are typically completed to achieve 100% inactivation of $6_{\log 10}$ *Geobacillus Stearothermophilus* BIs. In studies where high numbers of BIs are used then probabilities of atypical BI positives may be taken into account by statistics or additional study.

For security in condensation distribution a greater amount of H_2O_2 disinfectant is used than that used to achieve 6_{log10} inactivation of BIs. When setting cycle overkill the following process variables are considered.

1. The worst case RH% starting condition (lowest).
2. The worst case environment temperature starting condition (highest).
3. The temperature distribution on surfaces (location to location in the target area).
4. The gas distribution result from location to location, a study with chemical indicators.
5. Stainless steel carrier BIs typically have 1–2 minute System D-values, as verified in pre-qualification studies. There may be enhanced resistance on different material surfaces during actual processes (33, 34) e.g. a worst case of up to 4 minute system D-values. Cycle overkill can be determined using published studies, taking into account this variability.
6. Variation in peroxide amount delivered (grams vaporised).
7. Variation in other systems that impact on H_2O_2 vapour concentration or rate of rise to saturated vapour conditions e.g. circulating systems with HEPA filters.

Recommended cycle release criteria for sporicidal process quality assurance

The following release criteria checks are recommended to be added to the SOP for checking on the cycle printout, providing early indication of out-of-specification deviation before the final release quality control step:

1. Verify valid (expiry and weight) disinfectant agent was used.

2. Verify correct cycle program was used.
3. Verify the cycle was alarm free.
4. Check the gas concentration was above the defined alert level (set by trending results)
5. Verify the cycle print record is retained and signed or data logged in a secure system.

9.9 Summary of the challenges and expectations

Gaseous disinfection of barrier systems is driven by the intentions of the industry harmonised initiatives of Quality by Design (QbD) and Quality Risk Management (QRM); primarily that risks can be properly assessed and mitigated if process knowledge is in place, and that this will lead to improved quality.

Once a process is understood, often requiring characterisation studies to understand the critical control points and interactions with other parameters, then process control and monitoring can be established to achieve a repeatable and robust process, two key requirements of any critical process.

QCAs once defined, can be managed and risks can be mitigated during the processing cycle by continuous detection of deviation, ideally in real-time. Following the QbD initiative quality assurance in bio-decontamination processes is established in process design, there is not just reliance on environmental monitoring, which at this current time has limitations.

If you take a sample at a point in time this is just a small representation of the actual condition or status of contamination control. Continuous sampling and monitoring for bio-contamination would better indicate if bio-contamination was present in the environment. Currently continuous bio-contamination monitoring technology is not available. Under development is instantaneous microbiological detection (IMD) technology. This technology provides a high level of detection for all biologicals in the environment, yielding significantly more contamination counts than normally detected with standard samplers. However, it is difficult to differentiate all biologicals detected in an environment from those that are clinically or process significant, hence it is currently difficult to interpret the associated risks.

The extent of process knowledge, control and monitoring potential in gaseous disinfection fully supports the increasing requirements of aseptic processing and bioburden control. Today's challenge is cycle time optimisation; process efficiency is critical in more competitive environments and process down-time or turnaround time between campaigns is the focus. Gaseous disinfection cycles that are excessively long or material disinfection transfer steps that slow the process flow are no longer considered acceptable.

As more and more biological products are being developed, characterisation studies will be required to assess disinfection agent compatibility.

There is a clear balance to strike between managing bio-contamination (efficacy and repeatability of the process), and relative compatibilities between cleaning and disinfection technologies and medicinal, therapeutic or diagnostic products.

9.10 References

1. ISO 14644 Cleanrooms and associated controlled environments. Part (1) Classification of air cleanliness, International Standards Organisation, Geneva, Switzerland, 2015.
2. Euradlex. The Rules Governing Medicinal Products in the European Community, Annex 1, published by the European Commission, 2008.
3. Whyte, W. and Hejab, M. Particle and microbial airborne dispersion from people. *European Journal of Parenteral and Pharmaceutical sciences* 2007; 12 (2):39-40.
4. Midcalf, B., Mitchell Phillips, W., Neiger, J.S., Coles T .J, (Eds.). *Pharmaceutical Isolators: A guide to their application, design and control*. Pharmaceutical Press; 2004. (Yellow guide)
5. PHSS Technical monograph 15. Restricted Access Barrier Systems (RABS) Definition, Classification, Specification, and Use for Aseptic and Related Processing; 2011.
6. Lysfjord, J., Porter M. Barrier Isolation history and trends, a millennium update. *Pharm Eng* 2001; 21(2):142-5.
7. Porter, M., Lysfjord, J. Barrier Isolation history and trends, 2010 final data (presentation of ISPE Isolator survey results - completed yearly). Presented at the 27th ISPE Barrier Isolation conference; 2011 Chicago, USA.
8. FDA – Guide to Industry, Sterile drug products produced by Aseptic processing – Current Good Manufacturing Practice. Sept 2004.
9. European Pharmacopoeia (EP) 8th edition, 2015.

10. United States Pharmacopoeia (USP): 2015.
11. Biological indicators – PDA technical report 51. Biological Indicators for sporicidal gassing processes, PDA Technical report TR51; 2010.
12. Holmdahl, T., Lanbeck, P., Wullt, M., Walder, MH. A Head-to-Head Comparison of Hydrogen Peroxide Vapor and Aerosol Room Decontamination Systems. *Infection Control and Hospital Epidemiology* 2011; 32(9):831-6.
13. WHO classification of formaldehyde. International Agency for Research on Cancer, World Health Organisation (WHO) Press release No.153 15, June 2004 – IARC Classifies Formaldehyde as Carcinogenic to humans.
14. Johnston, M.D., Lawson, S., Otter, J.A. Evaluation of hydrogen peroxide vapour as a method for the decontamination of surfaces contaminated with *Clostridium botulinum* spores. *J. Microbiol. Methods*. 2005; 60:403-411.
15. Hall, L., Otter, J.A., Chewins, J., Wengenack, N.L. Use of hydrogen peroxide vapour for deactivation of *Mycobacterium tuberculosis* in a biological safety cabinet and a room. *J. Clin. Microbiol.* 2007; 45:810-815.
16. Otter, J.A., French, G.L. Survival of nosocomial bacteria and spores on surfaces and inactivation by hydrogen peroxide vapour (HPV). *J. Clin. Microbiol.* 2009; 47:205-207.
17. Otter, J.A., Chewins, C., Windsor, D., Windsor, H. Microbial contamination in cell culture: a potential role for hydrogen peroxide vapour (HPV)? *Cell. Biol. Int.* 2008; 32:326-327.
18. Otter, J.A., Budde-Niekiel. Hydrogen peroxide vapour: a novel method for the environmental

control of lactococcal bacteriophage. J. *Food. Protect.* 2009; 72:412-414.

19. Hall, L., Otter, J.A., Chewins, J. Wengenack, N.L. Deactivation of the dimorphic fungi *Histoplasma capsulatum, Blastomyces dermatitidis* and *Coccidioides immitis* using hydrogen peroxide vapor. *Med. Mycol.* 2008; 46:189-191.
20. Anipsitakis, G.A. & Dionysiou, D.D. Radical generation by the interaction of transition metals with common oxidants. *Environ. Sci. Technol.* 2004; 38, 3705-3712.
21. Block, S.S, editor. Peroxygen compounds in: *Disinfection, Sterilization and Preservation*, 5th ed. Philadelphia: Lippincott Williams & Wilkins. 2000; pp. 186-204.
22. Turner FJ. *Hydrogen peroxide and other oxidant disinfectants.* 3rd ed. Philadelphia: Lea Febiger 1983; 240-250.
23. Dean, R.T., Stocker, R., Davies, M.J. Biochemistry and pathology of radical-mediated protein oxidation. *Biochemistry.* 1997; 324:1–18.
24. Imlay, J.A. Pathways of oxidative damage. *Annu. Rev. Microbiol.* 2003; 57: 395-418.
25. Melly, E., Cowan, A.E., Setlow, P. Studies on the mechanism of killing *B. subtilis* spores by hydrogen peroxide. *J Appl. Microbiol.* 2002; 93:316–325.
26. Nakamura, K., Tamaoki, T. Reversible dissociation of *Escherichia coli* ribosomes by hydrogen peroxide. *Biochim. Biophys. Acta.* 1968; 23:368-376.
27. Denyer, S.P. Mechanisms of action of antibacterial biocides. *Int. Biodeter. Biodegrad.* 1995; 36: 227-245.
28. Selvaraj, R.J., Zgliczynski, J.M., Paul, B.B., Sbarra, A.J. Enhanced killing of myeloperoxidase-coated

bacteria in the myeloperoxidase-H_2O_2-Cl- system. *J. Infect. Dis*. 1978; 137:481-485.

29. Watling, D., Ryle, C., Parks M., Christopher M. Theoretical analysis of the condensation of hydrogen peroxide gas and water vapour as used in surface decontamination *PDA J Pharm Sci Journal* 2002; 56(6):291-9.
30. Unger-Bimczoz, B., Kottke, V., Hertel, C., Rauschnabel, J: The Influence of Humidity, Hydrogen peroxide Concentration and Condensation on the Inactivation of *Geobacillus stearothermophilus* Spores with Hydrogen Peroxide Vapor: *J. Pharm. Innov*. 2008; 3; 123-133.
31. Towne, V., Oswald, B., Mogg, R. *et al.* Measurement and Decomposition Kinetics of Residual Hydrogen Peroxide in the Presence of Commonly Used Excipients and Preservatives. *J Pharm Sci*. 2009; 98:3987-3996.
32. Drinkwater, J., Chewins, J., Steele, G. Biological Indicators don't lie, but in sporicidal gassing disinfection cycles do they sometimes confuse the truth? *European Journal of Parenteral and Pharmaceutical Sciences*. 2009; 14(1):5-10
33. Sigwarth, V, Stark A. Effect of carrier materials on resistance of spores of bacillus stearothermophilus to gaseous hydrogen peroxide. *PDA J Pharm. Sci. Journal*. 2003; 57(1):3-11.
34. Duthom, B. BIs for H_2 O_2 Bio-decontamination. Various Carrier Materials vs. Stainless steel only. Presented at the 14th ISPE Barrier Isolation Technology Forum; 2005 Arlington, USA.

CHAPTER 10:

VALIDATION OF DISINFECTANTS

By Tim Sandle

10.1 Introduction

An important aspect of the selection and evaluation of disinfectants is the disinfectant validation programme. After a disinfectant has been chosen based on its chemical properties and expected performance/ effectiveness (as outlined in chapter one), each disinfectant should be validated to ensure its efficacy (and for European Medicines Inspectorate and FDA regulated premises this is mandatory). Efficacy is demonstrated through performance testing to show that the disinfectant is capable of reducing the microbial bioburden in either suspension (planktonic state) or from cleanroom surfaces to an acceptable level. The disinfectant efficacy validation should provide documented evidence that the disinfectant demonstrates bactericidal, fungicidal, and/or sporicidal activity necessary to control microbial contamination in the facility. This chapter summarises the test requirements and the different standards that are currently available.

Regulatory agencies expect the users of disinfectants within cleanrooms to evaluate the efficacy of disinfectants. Various standards are available to guide the microbiologist through this process. What is more difficult is the content of some of the standards themselves because they have not been written specifically for the healthcare sector or the pharmaceutical industry (more typically they have evolved from the food, cosmetics or environmental control sectors). It may be necessary for the microbiologist to adapt the standards to suit practical situations (backing this up with a well-thought out rationale). Another point to be considered before embarking on such validation is whether all of the standards are to be replicated or whether experimental work required by some of the standards can be provided by the manufacturer of the disinfectants.

The chapter considers:

- Disinfection test standards
- An overview of the suspension test, surface test, and hand sanitisation tests.
- Consideration of differences between the major standards: the European (CEN) and USA (AOAC) approaches.

The reader should note that whilst 'field trials' are a component of disinfectant qualification, they are normally only performed in the pharmaceutical sector. As such, a discussion of field trials is contained within Chapter Eight.

10.2 Validation standards

Various standards are available to guide the microbiologist through the validation process. The particular methods chosen for the validation study depends on the needs of the facility and the intended use of the disinfectant. The following organizations publish disinfectant validation standards:

- ASTM (American Society for Testing Materials) (ASTM E2614 - 08 Standard Guide for Evaluation of Cleanroom Disinfectants)
- AOAC (Association of Official Analytical Chemists International) (referenced below)
- CEN (European Standards) (referenced below)
- TGA (Australian Therapeutic Goods Administration)
- USP (United States Pharmacopeia) (chapter <1072>)

The most widely used methods are the European CEN standards and the US AOAC standards, and it is these standards upon which the chapter focuses. The European approach consists of suspension tests, surface tests and field trials; whereas the emphasis in North America is strongly on surface testing (the Hard Surface Carrier Method). Here the carrier test differs slightly in methodology to the European surface Test (1)

10.3 Test requirements

The European standards for disinfectant efficacy were outlined by the European Committee for Standardisation Technical Committee 216 (CEN TC 216) in 1991, which began with guidance on disinfectant selection (EN 7152 24) and the first European disinfectant standard was issued in 1997: BS EN 1276 for the quantitative suspension test and several other standards then followed (2). These new standards replaced former methods for disinfectant validation, such as the once dominant Kelsey-Sykes test (3). For a full list of European disinfectant standards, refer to Appendix 1 of this chapter. The U.S. approach is less clear-cut, with ASTM, EPA and USP outlining different approaches. Appendix II lists some of these.

The standard approach for disinfectant validation consists of a basic suspension test, a quantitative suspension test (with low and high levels of organic material added to act as 'interfering substances') and a two-part simulated-use surface test. The standard European approach for disinfectant validation is divided up into three phases:

1. Phase 1 Basic Suspension Tests
2. Phase 2 Part 1: Suspension and surface tests to simulate practical usage: Bactericidal and fungicidal (sporicidal and virucidal)
3. Part 2: Surface test
4. Phase 3 Field Trial
5. A separate approach exists for the validation of hand sanitisers and hard surface wipes

The basic suspension test is a simple test to determine if the test disinfectant possesses any antimicrobial properties against microorganisms held in suspension (that is the microorganisms are added to the disinfectant solution). The quantitative suspension and surface tests are tests to determine the most effective concentration and conditions for the disinfectant as a simulation of practical conditions. The field trials show the effectiveness of a chosen disinfectant *in-loco* conditions (the pharmaceutical cleanrooms). With each stage an important consideration is the selection of an appropriate neutraliser. A neutraliser counter acts on any residual disinfectant and allows microorganisms to be recovered which might otherwise have been inhibited.

10.4 Basic suspension test

Phase 1 - Basic Suspension Test (Standards EN 1275 and EN 1040)

A suspension test is a test designed to measure the efficacy of a disinfectant against selected microorganisms in the planktonic state after a predetermined contact time. Two standards are published within Europe in order to examine this: EN 1040 to measure bactericidal activity and EN 1275 to measure fungicidal activity. The basic suspension test is a simple, limited test of the product and is performed in order to determine minimum standards. In many ways the basic suspension test only serves to confirm the manufacturer's data within the testing laboratory. Indeed, many facilities elect to audit the manufacturer and to review the manufacturer's data in lieu of conducting the basic suspension test at their own premises.

Before undertaking the test, the selection of a suitable sterile neutraliser is required. Selection involves spiking neutralisers of different activity with a range of microorganisms and measuring the recovery. The neutraliser with the optimal recovery should be selected. Some neutralisers have general properties, such as, lecithin. Other neutralisers are compatible with specific disinfectants, such as, polysorbate-80 for biguanides and sodium thiosulphate for hypochlorites.

The test evaluates the activity of a disinfectant against a range of microorganisms under conditions which simulate use. After challenging a disinfectant solution with a microbial population the mixture is plated out, after the required contact time, and the surviving microorganisms enumerated. No organic material is introduced to this test, unlike the quantitative suspension test described below. In addition to the microorganisms prescribed in the standards, the microbiologist may elect to include representative organisms isolated from the cleanroom environment.

10.5 Quantitative suspension test

Phase 2, step 1 - Bactericidal suspension test (Standard: EN 1276) and *Fungicidial suspension test* (Standard EN 1650)

The purpose of the quantitative suspension test is to evaluate the activity of a disinfectant against a range of microorganisms under conditions which more closely simulate practical use. The practical conditions make the test more sophisticated than the basic suspension test. The test consists of adding a test suspension of bacteria or fungi to a prepared sample of the disinfectant under test in simulated 'clean' and 'dirty' conditions. After a specified contact time an aliquot is taken and the bactericidal / fungicidal action is immediately neutralised by the addition of a proven neutralizer (as identified in the basic suspension test). Following this, the number of surviving microorganisms in each sample is determined and the reduction in viable counts is calculated (expressed in logarithms to base 10).

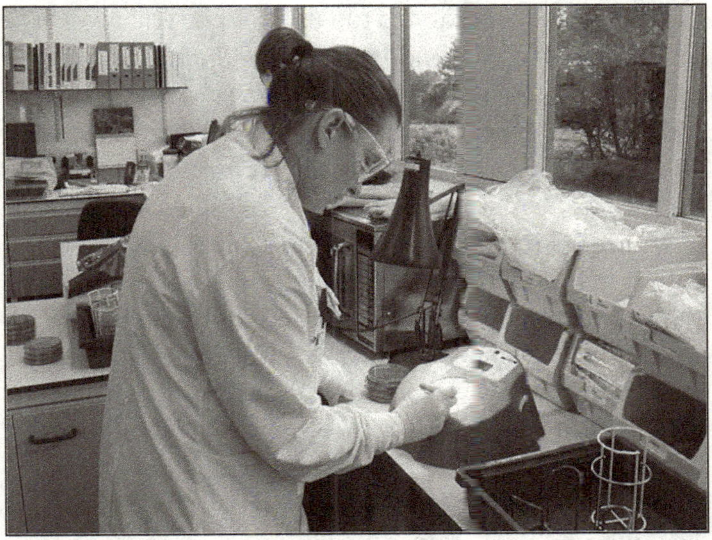

Figure 1: Examination of disinfectant test plates for microbial count (© Tim Sandle)

To achieve neutralisation the standard recommends dilution but if this is ineffective then membrane filtration may be used where the filter may trap microorganisms but filter through the disinfectant by the application of rinse solutions. Thus dilution; addition of a chemical neutralizer, and membrane filtration are the three standard methods for inactivation of antimicrobials (4).

The suspension test permits challenges of different concentrations of the disinfectant against a range of set test microorganisms. The concentrations need to be constructed to cover the manufacturer's recommendations for the active and non-active ranges. This is to demonstrate whether the manufacturer's recommended concentration is effective and to understand the margin of failure (where the disinfectant solution is too dilute to be effective). The set organisms are: *Pseudomonas aeruginosa*, *Escherichia coli*, *Staphylococcus aureus* and *Enterococcus faecium / hirae*, for the bactericidal test, and *Aspergillus niger* and *Candida albicans* for the fungicidal test. The bactericidal standard also makes provision for additional microorganisms to be used in specific industries. These are: *Salmonella typhimurium* (which would be used for the food industry), *Lactobacillus brevis* (which would be used for breweries) and *Enterobacter cloacae*. To achieve a 'pass', the concentration of disinfectant, at a temperature of 20°C and a contact time of 5 minutes, must produce a minimum five log reduction of the challenge bacteria and a minimum of a four log reduction for the challenge fungi. The time and temperature may be varied depending upon the application, although once established the disinfectant should not be used outside of the verified ranges.

In addition to the standard, it would seem that many regulatory inspectors would expect the inclusion of environmental isolates found from the manufacturing environment. The addition of spore bearing microorganisms can also be introduced to challenge disinfectants with sporicidal properties. Research from Payne *et al* (5) indicates that of all of the test microorganisms it is *Pseudomonas aeruginosa* that is generally the most resistant.

In addition to testing the differing concentrations, the standard also requires that the disinfectant is made up in the 'worst case' condition by using 'water of standard hardness' (which contains ions like magnesium and calcium, as well as other salts). A further condition is the simulation of 'soiling', by the addition of bovine serum albumin (at 0.03%, representing 'clean' conditions and at 0.3% representing 'dirty' conditions). Some manufacturers will also introduce an additional organic load, which is representative of residues likely to be found within their cleanrooms, as well as other in-use temperatures and variations to contact times from one to sixty minutes.

10.6 Surface tests

Phase 2, step 2 - surface test (Standards EN 13713 and EN 13697) and AOAC standard AOAC 991.47 Hard surface carrier test method.

Surface tests are sometimes referred to as carrier tests. It is at this stage that the European and US disinfection tests have a level of similarity. With surface tests, representative manufacturing surface samples are inoculated with a selection of microbial challenge organisms. A disinfectant is applied to the inoculated surfaces and exposed for a predetermined contact time after which the surviving organisms are recovered using a qualified disinfectant-neutralizing broth and test method (surface rinse, contact plate, or swab). The number of challenge organisms recovered from the test samples (exposed to a disinfectant) is compared to the number of challenge organisms recovered from the corresponding control sample (not exposed to a disinfectant) to determine the ability of the disinfectant to reduce the microbial bioburden. Successful completion of the validation qualifies the disinfectant evaluated for use.

Prior to initiating disinfectant efficacy validation, a comprehensive survey of the materials comprising the room surfaces (floors, walls, windows) and equipment (stainless steel, acrylic, vinyl) present in the facility which could potentially be exposed to the disinfectant should be conducted. The use of different surfaces is important because the rates of inactivation on microorganisms on different surfaces can vary considerably. One study demonstrated that bactericidal activity reduced on PVC compared with stainless steel. This was a factor both of the material type and the surface conditions, such as, the number of pores or ridges. Surfaces of the material can also differ depending upon the degree of finishing with smoother surfaces, like stainless steel or Formica, giving greater repeatability and reproducibility (6).

Most facilities will not use every type of surface but instead will select the most common types of surfaces. Should this bracketing strategy be employed, it is crucial that the rationale for surface selection be detailed in the efficacy validation protocol as regulators will seek evidence that representative surfaces have been challenged. Once appropriate surfaces have been selected, 2" × 2" coupons of the surface material should be obtained. These coupons, referred to as "surface carriers," serve as the representative surfaces for the testing (7).

The European standards that describe the test are EN 13713, for the basic surface test, and EN 13697, for a quantitative surface test, which includes the presence of interfering substances. The standards are largely similar to previous German DGHM methods. The surface test is based on the suspension test with the variable parameters of interfering substances, temperature and contact time. However, the required log reduction differs from the

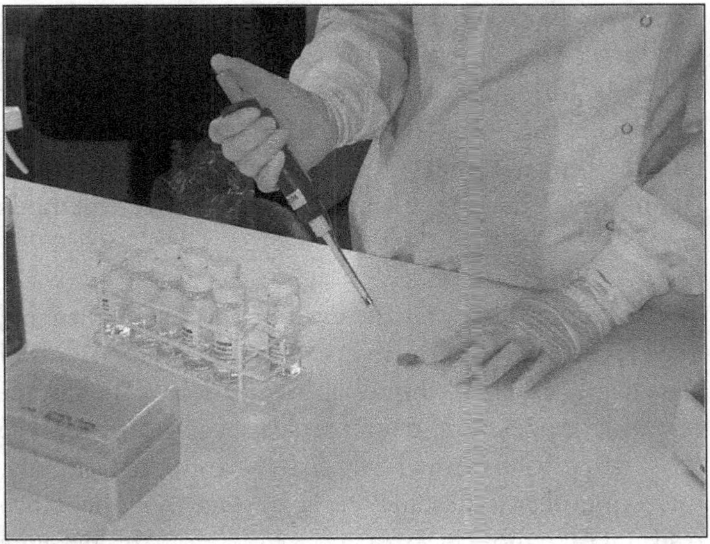

Figure 2: Inoculating coupons for the disinfectant surface test (© Tim Sandle)

suspension test in that, to pass, a 4 log decrease for bacteria and a 3 log decrease for fungi must be obtained The required test organisms are identical to the suspension test: *Pseudomonas aeruginosa*, *Escherichia coli*, *Staphylococcus aureus*, *Enterococcus hirae*, *Aspergillus niger* and *Candida albicans*. For this test, fungi are incorporated within the one standard. The microbiologist will also consider the inclusion of environmental isolates and spore bearing microorganisms (arguments as to when an environmental isolate becomes a 'laboratory culture' and problems in creating adequate spore suspensions notwithstanding (8)

With the AOAC use-dilution test (a carrier-based test), the organisms used are: *Salmonella cholerasuis*,

Staphylococcus aureus and *Pseudomonas aeruginosa*. The principles are generally similar to the European methods but there are some variations. For specific details on the AOAC methods, these are detailed in AOAC International Official Methods of Analysis, Arlington, VA. The European and AOAC methods vary.

The surface test is by far the most important, challenging and representative of the tests of disinfectant efficacy and this chapter examines this test in greater detail. The surface test is more relevant than the suspension test because it is truer to practical conditions and theoretically, microorganisms attached to a surface will be more resistant than those in a suspension, therefore this presents the greatest challenge. The quantitative surface test evaluates test suspensions of bacteria and fungi in a solution of interfering substances, designed to simulate clean and dirty conditions, which are inoculated onto a test surface and dried. The test aims to acquire quantitative information about the ability of a disinfectant to kill microorganisms attached to hard surfaces.

The test works by examining preparations of microorganisms dried onto surfaces. To such a dried suspension, a prepared sample of the disinfectant is added. The surface is then transferred to a previously validated neutralisation medium and tests performed to measure the reduction in viable counts. The test involves drying 0.05 ml suspensions of the microorganisms (with interfering substances such as bovine serum albumin) onto different surfaces. The microorganisms should have a population range of 1.5 =n 5.0 × 10^8 for bacteria and 1.5 =n 5.0 × 10^7

for fungi and are equilibrated to 25°C before use. Once applied to the surface the drying of the microorganisms may be accelerated using an incubator operating at 36-38°C. Disinfectant solutions (where disinfectants are made with Water of Standard Hardness) are added to the surfaces. After the specified contact time (five minutes is the target) the surfaces are transferred to the validated neutralisation medium and then pour plates are prepared for incubation and counting. An alternative method is available using a soaked swab step (9)

A variation of the surface test involves the use of mechanical action. Mechanical action is more akin to practical conditions (such as the application of a cloth or a mop). However, the more efficacious disinfectants do not require any mechanical action when the disinfectant and the surface come into contact. For the surface test, mechanical action is very difficult to reproduce. It is preferable to evaluate a disinfectant without mechanical action and this aspect can be examined during the Phase 3 field trials. Furthermore, mechanical action is a very variable procedure and is difficult to evaluate.

It may arise that the disinfectant concentration shown to be optimal for the suspension test needs to be increased to meet the requirements of the surface test. The suspension test has further weaknesses in that it enhances the potential for small dilution errors made in the preparation of disinfectant solutions in relation to the final pass or fail result. The suspension test has been shown to be difficult to reproduce both between and within laboratories and often lacks precision. The suspension test can also pose problems when disinfectants with a high viscosity are challenged due to their distribution in the test suspension (10).

The surface test, however, cannot demonstrate the effect of a range of environmental factors like temperature, pH, detergent residues, mechanical stress and attachment. For these reasons a disinfectant which appears effective for the surface test can show marked variability when applied to practical conditions. The reasons for this are due to problems in drying and differences between surfaces. In terms of drying microbial suspensions, there is a marked loss in the viability of a population when dried onto a surface and attempts to speed the drying process up do not significantly reduce the variability of the actual number of microorganisms challenged. Surfaces introduce another variation because surfaces, even of the same grade of material, are not truly identical and there have been marked problems in achieving reproducibility and repeatability for the surface test between laboratories particularly in estimating the concentration of disinfectant required to be effective (11). Some of these limitations can be addressed through field trials.

10.7 Wipes

In Europe, the test for pre-saturated disinfectant wipes is outlined in EN 16615. This standard is a practice-like test for the efficacy testing of wipes. The test uses a large carrier (20 x 50 cm). With this the impregnated wipe is applied with a standardised procedure to simulate the disinfection of small surfaces. The standard recommends the so-termed "4-field-test" approach to be used. The name comes from the fact that in this test assay not only the disinfecting efficacy on a contaminated surface is tested, but also the spread to other parts of the carrier. This will be tested on the remaining 3 fields, which have not been contaminated upfront.

In the U.S., the EPA has an alternative method. This is the pre-saturated towelette disinfection test method. With the method, a 48 hour culture of an individual species of bacteria is dried onto a number of clean, sterile glass test surfaces (microscope slides). The test can include an "organic soil load" if required.

The dry, contaminated test surfaces are placed in Petri dishes and then wiped, individually, with the pre-saturated towelettes in accordance with manufacturer instructions and in light of EPA guidance regarding the number of test surfaces that must be treated with a single pre-saturated towelette. Typically 60 contaminated test surfaces are treated in total with the pre-saturated disinfectant towelettes. After the test surfaces are wiped with the towelette, they are allowed to rest (usually in a Petri dish) for the remainder of the contact time. After the contact time has elapsed, the treated test surfaces are transferred, individually at intervals, to sterile test tubes or jars containing a liquid growth medium that has been amended with chemical agents to immediately neutralize the action of the disinfectant present on the pre-saturated towelette.

After transfer from the disinfectant, the treated test surfaces are incubated in the neutralizing growth medium for 48 hours. After incubation, the number of tubes showing growth of the target microorganism is recorded. To "pass" a 60 carrier test, at least 59 of the 60 surfaces wiped with the towelettes must demonstrate complete disinfection (no detectable growth of the target microorganism in the test tubes containing neutralizing growth medium).

10.8 Culture Media

Once the neutraliser used in the suspension and surface tests has been established, it is important that the neutraliser is incorporated into the culture media used to perform cleanroom environmental monitoring. If the media is used without neutraliser or with an inappropriate neutraliser, then the results of environmental monitoring will be an underestimation of the microbial population from the cleanroom surface. Where disinfectants are used in rotation it is preferable to use a universal neutraliser in the culture medium rather than to use different culture media with different formulations for monitoring campaigns.

Figure 3: Counting plates from cleanroom monitoring (© Tim Sandle)

10.9 Hand sanitisation

Hand sanitisation (Standard: EN 1500)

An associated part of disinfectant evaluation is the assessment of hand sanitisers. There are many commercially available hand sanitisers, with the most commonly used types being alcohol-based gels. Within Europe there is a standard describing the approach for the validation of hand sanitisers based on two norms: EN1499 (hygienic hand wash), and EN 1500 (hygienic hand disinfection). It is more typical for the EN 1500 standard to be followed. Many commercially available hand sanitisers are surprisingly difficult to test against the standard in terms of effectively reducing microbial populations and several types have compared unfavourably to straightforward hand washing with simple soaps. Some alcohols are more effective than others, based on their molecular weight. The alcohol 1-propanol (C_3H_8O)[7] is used as the test standard against which hand sanitisers are compared (12).

The test for hand sanitisers can be applied to skin and to gloved hands. One problem with the application to gloved hands is that the gloves themselves may either carry a microbial load or be prone to leaks. Some material, such as latex, can trap microorganisms onto the surface. These factors can reduce the reliability of the test results (13).

---

[7] An isomer of isopropanol (2-propanol), that is a compound with the same molecular formula but with a different structural formula.

The test determines if a hand sanitiser can reduce the number of transient microflora under simulated practical conditions. The hand sanitiser under test is compared against a reference standard (60% propan-1-ol) using fifteen test subjects. For tests of gloved hands, several microorganisms can be selected. However, only one microorganism can be used for the study on human skin for health and safety considerations: *Eschericia coli* K12 (ATCC 10538[8]) which is a non-pathogenic Class I microorganism under Directive 90/679 EEC. To be effective the test hand sanitiser must produce a five log reduction of the test microorganism. The agar plates used to measure recovery contain the additive 0.5g/l of sodium desoxycholate in order to inhibit the growth of any skin *Staphylococci*.

The act of agitation and rubbing the hand sanitiser into the skin or into the glove presents the greatest variable into the test. This is partly, but not completely, overcome by the large subject size but difficulties exist in comparing different laboratories. For practical use there is a significant effect on the survival of microflora based on the frequency of application, the degree of hand rubbing and the quantity applied (14, 15).

10.10 Continuing evaluation of disinfectants

The continued efficacy of the disinfectants should be assessed to verify that they remain effective in controlling

8 Strain K-12 was isolated at Stanford University in 1922 from human faeces.

microbial contamination. As part of this assessment, a record of microbial isolates identified in the facility should be tracked and trended on a periodic basis to identify:

- The most frequently isolated organisms,
- Atypical microbial isolates,
- Isolates associated with continued adverse trends,
- Isolates associated with both environmental/personnel and product bioburden.

When unusual isolates are recovered, or where there is repeated isolation of theoretically more resistant microorganisms (as described in chapter one), it may be prudent to challenge such isolates against one or more of the disinfectant test methods outlined in this chapter.

10.11 Summary

This chapter has outlined the approaches which can be taken for the evaluation of disinfectants. The chapter has indicated that the standard adopted depends upon the application, what the user wishes to demonstrate and the applicable regulatory body. In terms of the objective of validation: to ensure that the in-use disinfectant is the most effective, then for this the surface tests are the most meaningful tests to conduct. The suspension test has been shown to be difficult to reproduce both between and within laboratories and often lacks precision. The suspension test has further weaknesses in that it enhances the potential for small dilution errors made in the preparation of disinfectant solutions in relation to the final pass or fail result. The suspension test can also pose problems when disinfectants with a high viscosity are challenged due to their distribution in the test suspension (6).

Some of the key considerations for disinfectant validation are summarised in the diagram below:

There are many important aspects to take into account for disinfectant validation. Arguably the most important is that disinfectants should be evaluated under simulated-use conditions, integrating the net effects of disinfectant preparation, concentration, application and contact time with different challenge organisms and surface properties.

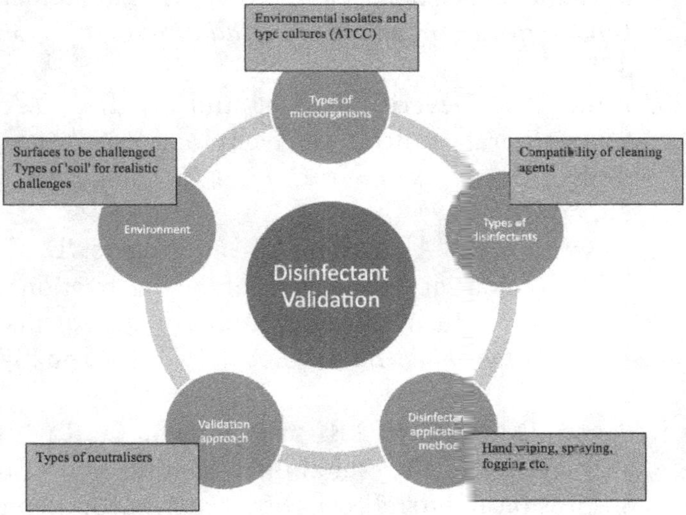

Figure 4: Diagram summarising some of the key aspects to consider for disinfectant validation (© Tim Sandle)

10.12 References

1. Reybrouck, G.: 'The testing of disinfectants', *International Biodeterioration and Biodegradation*, 41, 1998, pp269-272
2. Holah, J. T. Progress report on CEN TC 216 WG3: Disinfectant test methods for food hygiene - institutional and domestic applications, *International Biodeterioration and Biodegradation*, 1997, 36, 355 – 365
3. Prince, J., Deverill, C.E.A. and Ayliffe, G.A.: 'A membrane filtration technique for testing disinfectants', *Journal of Clinical Pathology*, 1975, 28, pp71-76
4. Russell, A.D., Ahonkhai, I. And Rogers, D. T.: 'Microbiological Applications of the Inactivation of Antibiotics and Other Antimicrobial Agents', *Journal of Applied Bacteriology*, 1979, 46, pp207-245
5. Payne, D.N., Babb, J.R. and Bradley, C. R.: 'An evaluation of the suitability of the European Suspension Test to reflect in vitro activity of antiseptic against clinically chosen significant organisms', *Letters in Applied Microbiology*, 1999, 28, pp7-12
6. Bloomfield, S.F., Arthur, M., Van Klingeren, B., Pullen, W., Holah, J.T. and Elton, R.: 'An evaluation of the repeatability and reproducibility of a surface test for the activity of disinfectants', *Journal of Applied Bacteriology*, 1994, 76, pp86-94
7. Vina, P., Rubio, S. and Sandle, T. (2011): 'Selection and Validation of Disinfectants', in Saghee, M.R., Sandle, T. and Tidswell, E.C. (Eds.) (2011): *Microbiology and Sterility Assurance in Pharmaceuticals and Medical Devices*, New Delhi: Business Horizons, pp219-236

8. Russell, A. D.: 'Assessment of sporicidal efficacy', *International Biodeterioration and Biodegradation*, 41, 1998, pp281-287
9. van Kilgeren, B., Koller, W., Bloomfield, S.F., Bohm, R., Cremieux, A, Holah, J., Reybrouck, G. and Rodger, H-J.: 'Assessment of the efficacy of disinfectants on surfaces', *International Biodeterioration and Biodegradation*, 41, 1998, pp289-296
10. Bloomfield, S. F., Arthur, M., Begun, K. and Patel, H.: 'Comparative testing of disinfectants using proposed European surface test methods', *Letters in Applied Microbiology*, 1993, 17, pp119-125
11. Langsrud, S. and Sundheim, G.: 'Factors influencing a suspension test method for antimicrobial activity of disinfectants', *Journal of Applied Microbiology*, 1998, 85, pp1006-1012
12. Kramer, A., Rudolph P., Kampf, G. and Pittet, D. (2002): 'Limited efficacy of alcohol-based hand gels', *The Lancet*, Vol. 359, April 27th 2002.
13. Best, M. and Kennedy, M.E.: 'Effectiveness of handwashing agents in eliminating Staphylococcus aureus from gloved hands', *Journal of Applied Bacteriology*, 1992, 73, pp63-66
14. Namura, S., Nishijima, S., McGinley, J. and Leyden, J.: 'A study of the efficacy of antimicrobial detergents for handwashing: using the full-hand touch plates method', *The Journal of Dermatology*, 1993, Vol. 20, pp88-93
15. Larson, E., Mayur, K. and Laughon, B.: 'Influence of two handwashing frequencies on reduction in colonizing flora with three handwashing products used by health care personnel', *American Journal of Infection Control*, 1989, Vol. 17, No.2, pp83-88

APPENDIX 1: LIST OF EUROPEAN DISINFECTANT STANDARDS

Note: not all of these standards are applicable to pharmaceutical manufacturing or to healthcare (the most applicable chapters to this book have been discussed within).

- EN 14347:2005: Chemical disinfectants and antiseptics - Basic sporicidal activity - Test method and requirements (phase 1)
- EN 13704:2007: Chemical disinfectants - Quantitative suspension test for the evaluation of sporicidal activity of chemical disinfectants used in food, industrial, domestic and institutional areas - Test method and requirements (phase 2, step 1)
- EN 1499:2013: Chemical disinfectants and antiseptics - Hygienic handwash - Test method and requirements (phase 2/step 2)
- EN 1500:2013: Chemical disinfectants and antiseptics - Hygienic handrub - Test method and requirements (phase 2/step 2)
- EN 12791:2005: Chemical disinfectants and antiseptics - Surgical hand disinfection - Test method and requirement (phase 2/step 2)
- EN 16615:2015: Chemical disinfectants and antiseptics. Quantitative test method for the evaluation of bactericidal and yeasticidal activity on

non-porous surfaces with mechanical action employing wipes in the medical area (4- field test). Test method and requirements (phase 2, step 2)

- EN 14204:2012: Chemical disinfectants and antiseptics - Quantitative suspension test for the evaluation of mycobactericidal activity of chemical disinfectants and antiseptics used in the veterinary area - Test method and requirements (phase 2, step 1)
- EN 14675:2015: Chemical disinfectants and antiseptics - Quantitative suspension test for the evaluation of virucidal activity of chemical disinfectants and antiseptics used in the veterinary area - Test method and requirements (phase 2, step 1)
- EN 13610:2002: Chemical disinfectants - Quantitative suspension test for the evaluation of virucidal activity against bacteriophages of chemical disinfectants used in food and industrial areas - Test method and requirements (phase 2, step 1)
- EN 13697:2015: Chemical disinfectants and antiseptics - Quantitative non-porous surface test for the evaluation of bactericidal and/or fungicidal activity of chemical disinfectants used in food, industrial, domestic and institutional areas - Test method and requirements without mechanical action (phase 2/step2)
- EN 13727:2013: Chemical disinfectants and antiseptics - Quantitative suspension test for the evaluation of bactericidal activity of chemical disinfectants for instruments used in the medical area - Test method and requirements (phase 2, step 1)
- EN 13624:2013: Chemical disinfectants and antiseptics - Quantitative suspension test for the

evaluation of fungicidal activity of chemical disinfectants for instruments used in the medical area - Test method and requirements (phase 2, step 1)

- EN 14561:2006: Chemical disinfectants and antiseptics - Quantitative carrier test for the evaluation of bactericidal activity for instruments used in the medical area - Test method and requirements (phase 2, step 2)
- EN 14562:2006: Chemical disinfectants and antiseptics - Quantitative carrier test for the evaluation of fungicidal or yeasticidal activity for instruments used in the medical area - Test method and requirements (phase 2, step 2)
- EN 14563:2008: Chemical disinfectants and antiseptics - Quantitative carrier test for the evaluation of mycobactericidal or tuberculocidal activity of chemical disinfectants used for instruments in the medical area - Test method and requirements (phase 2, step 2)
- EN 14348:2005: Chemical disinfectants and antiseptics - Quantitative suspension test for the evaluation of mycobactericidal activity of chemical disinfectants in the medical area including instrument disinfectants - Test methods and requirements (phase 2, step 1)
- EN 14885:2006: Chemical disinfectants and antiseptics - Application of European Standards for chemical disinfectants and antiseptics
- EN 12353:2013: Chemical disinfectants and antiseptics - Preservation of test organisms used for the determination of bactericidal, mycobactericidal, sporicidal and fungicidal activity

- EN 1275:2005: Chemical disinfectants and antiseptics - Quantitative suspension test for the evaluation of basic fungicidal or basic yeasticidal activity of chemical disinfectants and antiseptics - Test method and requirements (phase 1)
- EN 1040:2005: Chemical disinfectants and antiseptics - Quantitative suspension test for the evaluation of basic bactericidal activity of chemical disinfectants and antiseptics - Test method and requirements (phase 1)
- EN 1657:2005: Chemical disinfectants and antiseptics - Quantitative suspension test for the evaluation of fungicidal or yeasticidal activity of chemical disinfectants and antiseptics used in the veterinary area - Test method and requirements (phase 2, step 1)
- EN 14349:2012: Chemical disinfectants and antiseptics - Quantitative surface test for the evaluation of bactericidal activity of chemical disinfectants and antiseptics used in veterinary area on non-porous surfaces without mechanical action - Test method and requirements (phase 2, step 2)
- EN 14476:2013: Chemical disinfectants and antiseptics - Virucidal quantitative suspension test for chemical disinfectants and antiseptics used in human medicine - Test method and requirements (phase 2, step 1)
- EN 13623:2010: Chemical disinfectants and antiseptics - Quantitative suspension test for the evaluation of bactericidal activity against Legionella of chemical disinfectants for aqueous systems - Test method and requirements (phase 2, step 1)

- EN 1650:2013: Chemical disinfectants and antiseptics - Quantitative suspension test for the evaluation of fungicidal or yeasticidal activity of chemical disinfectants and antiseptics used in food, industrial, domestic and institutional areas - Test method and requirements (phase 2, step 1)
- EN 1276:2009: Chemical disinfectants and antiseptics - Quantitative suspension test for the evaluation of bactericidal activity of chemical disinfectants and antiseptics used in food, industrial, domestic and institutional areas - Test method and requirements (phase 2, step 1)
- EN 1656:2009: Chemical disinfectants and antiseptics - Quantitative suspension test for the evaluation of bactericidal activity of chemical disinfectants and antiseptics used in the veterinary area - Test method and requirements (phase 2, step 1)
- EN 1657:2005: Chemical disinfectants and antiseptics - Quantitative suspension test for the evaluation of fungicidal or yeasticidal activity of chemical disinfectants and antiseptics used in the veterinary area - Test method and requirements (phase 2, step 1)
- EN 1276:2009: Chemical disinfectants and antiseptics - Quantitative suspension test for the evaluation of bactericidal activity of chemical disinfectants and antiseptics used in food, industrial, domestic and institutional areas - Test method and requirements (phase 2, step 1)
- EN 1656:2009: Chemical disinfectants and antiseptics - Quantitative suspension test for the evaluation of bactericidal activity of chemical disinfectants and antiseptics used in the veterinary area - Test method and requirements (phase 2, step 1)

APPENDIX 2: U.S. DISINFECTANT STANDARDS

In the U.S., publications or regulatory guidance/standards such as Chapter <1072>, "Disinfectants and Antiseptics" in the United States Pharmacopeia address the issue of disinfectant testing but do not state which method to use. For methods, those issued by the AOAC (Association Of Analytical Communities) tend to be followed, although this is not mandatory. Other sources include the U.S. EPA (Environmental Protection Agency) and the ASTM (American Society for Testing and Materials).

Types of disinfection methods include the following:

1. AOAC Use-dilution method.
2. AOAC Hard surface carrier test method.
3. AOAC Germicidal Spray Products.
4. ASTM Standards E2111, Standard Quantitative Carrier Test Method to Evaluate the Bactericidal, Fungicidal, Mycobactericidal, and Sporicidal Potencies of Liquid Chemical Microbicides.
5. ASTM Standards E2197 Standard Quantitative Disk Carrier Test Method for Determining the Bactericidal, Virucidal, Fungicidal Mycobactericidal and Sporicidal Activities of Liquid Chemical Germicides.

6. ASTM Standards E2315 Standard Guide for Assessment of Antimicrobial Activity Using a Time-Kill Procedure.
7. ASTM BS EN13697 Chemical Disinfectants and Antiseptics. Quantitative Non-Porous Surface Test for the Evaluation of Bactericidal and/or Fungicidal Activity of Chemical Disinfectants used in Food, Industrial, Domestic and Institutional Areas.

CLEANING AND DISINFECTION GLOSSARY

Compiled by Tim Sandle

Active Ingredient – The chemical component of a disinfectant that inactivates, reduces or destroys microorganisms.

Agar - A gelatinous material, extracted from seaweed, that is used to form the solid base for bacteriological culture medium.

Antibacterial - A chemical substance which kills bacteria.

Antimicrobial agent - a chemical that kills or inhibits the growth of microorganisms e.g. a disinfectant

Antiseptics - chemical agent used on exposed body surface to destroy or inhibit vegetative pathogens. It is the alternative name for sanitiser as in 'hand sanitiser'. The process of using such an agent is called antisepsis.

Asepsis - The absence of microorganisms that cause disease; freedom of infection; exclusion of microorganisms

Aseptic technique- manipulating sterile instruments, equipment or culture media in such a way as to avoid contamination.

Bacteria - Single-cell microorganisms.

Bactericidal - having the characteristic of destroying bacteria

Bactericide - An agent that kills bacteria.

Bacteriostat - a chemical or physical agent that inhibits the growth of, but is not lethal to bacteria.

Bacteriostatic - From the Greek words stasis and static means to stand still. A bacteriostatic agent prevents the growth of bacteria on tissue or on objects in the environment. Some disinfectants have bacteriostatic properties (as opposed to bactericidal).

Bioburden – a 'catch all phrase' that refers to the total microbial load of a sample or system. It normally infers unwanted contamination but can refer to the 'natural bioburden' or a substance.

Biofilm- Microbial cells encased in an adhesive, usually a polysaccharide material secreted by the community, and attached to a surface. They have complex structural and functional characteristics. Biofilms have physical/chemical gradients that influence microbial metabolic processes. They can form on inanimate devices (e.g. pipes) and also cause fouling (e.g. water systems). Often occurs at a physical e.g. water – solid interface.

CFU - Colony Forming Units. A measure of the number of microorganisms on an agar medium.

Cleanroom - a room in which the concentration of airborne particles is controlled to a defined standard. This is achieved by controlling the introduction, formation and retention of particles

Clean zone - a defined space within a cleanroom where the concentration of airborne particles is controlled. Often this is to a higher standard than the cleanroom.

Colony forming unit (CFU) - Colony forming units. Viable micro-organisms (bacteria, yeasts & mould) capable of growth under the prescribed conditions (medium, atmosphere, time and temperature) develop into visible colonies (colony forming units) which are counted. The term colony forming unit (CFU) is used because a colony may result from a single micro-organism or from a clump / cluster of micro-organisms. It is normally expressed as CFU per g or mL.

Contact Time - The time that a disinfectant or sanitising chemical must remain wet on the surface being treated.

Contaminant – a foreign agent not introduced as part of processing, such as airborne particulates or adventitious micro-organisms.

Contaminated - possessing infectious organisms or substances

Culture medium - an aqueous solution of various nutrients suitable for the growth of microorganisms. See media.

Decontamination - to make safe by removing or reducing contamination by infectious organisms or other harmful substances. It does not imply that all micro-organisms have been eliminated to zero count.

Degradation – loss or reduction of quality, integrity or character; or a reaction that breaks something down into smaller parts.

Detergent - an organic molecule, other than a soap, that serves as a wetting agent and emulsifier; it is normally used as cleanser, but some may be used as antimicrobial agents (this is more often called a **Disinfectant-Detergent:** a chemical product that is formulated with cleaning agents and biocides, selected for soil removal and simultaneous disinfection).

Disinfectant - an agent that kills all growing or vegetative forms of microorganisms, thus completely eliminating them from inanimate objects.

Disinfection - refers to the use of a physical process or a chemical agent (such as disinfectants) to destroy vegetative pathogens but not necessarily bacterial endospores

Ecosystem – a self-regulating biological community in a defined habitat

Efficacy – the ability of a substance (e.g. chemical disinfectant) to produce a desired effect (e.g. reduction in bacterial numbers) under different conditions.

Endospore- Differentiated cell formed within the cells of certain Gram-positive bacteria and extremely resistant to heat and other harmful agents. Sometimes simplified to 'spore'.

Environmental monitoring – a documented series of sampling and testing in controlled environments in order to demonstrate conformance to a series of pre-set limits or for trends. It is distinct from environmental control.

Filter – a porous material through which a liquid or gas is passed so that particulates and impurities and micro-organisms are held in suspension. Some 'impurities' will pass through depending upon the filter size, viscosity, concentration and so on. The part of the mixture that passes through is the filtrate.

Formulation – the method and process for selecting the components of a mixture, including the active ingredients, to make the form that the finished product (such as a disinfectant).

Fumigant- liquid or solid chemical which forms vapours that kill organisms.

Fungicide- chemical or physical agent that kills or inhibits development of fungus spores or mycelium. The term 'fungicide' includes all preparations intended for preventing, destroying, repelling or mitigating any fungi.

Fungistasis - Suppression of germination of fungal spores or other resting structures in natural soils as a result of competition for available nutrients, presence of inhibitory compounds, or both.

Fungistasis- The prevention of fungal growth; the effect is reversible, if the inhibitor is removed or diluted, growth is resumed.

Fungistatic - Able to inhibit germination of fungus spores or development of mycelium without causing death of fungus.

Good Manufacturing Practice (GMP) and current Good Manufacturing Practice (cGMP) – standards which relate to the manufacturing of biopharmaceuticals and blood products. Include SOPs to be followed; processes to be validated; equipment to be qualified; staff to be trained; and a clean environment to be maintained.

Gram-negative cell - a bacterial cell whose cell wall contains relatively little peptidogylcan but has an outer membrane composed of lipopolysaccharide, lipoprotein, and other complex macromolecules. Gram-negative and positive micro-organisms are distinguished using the Gram stain. Gram-negative micro-organisms do not retain the primary stain (crystal violet) and require counter-staining.

Gram-positive cell - a bacterial cell whose cell wall consists mainly of peptidogylcan and lacks the outer cell membrane found on Gram-negative cells. Gram-positive micro-organisms retain the primary stain (crystal violet).

Gram's stain - Differential stain that divides bacteria into two groups, Gram-positive and Gram-negative, based on the ability to retain crystal violet when decolorized with an organic solvent such as ethanol. The cell wall of Gram-positive bacteria consists chiefly of peptidoglycan and lacks the outer membrane of Gram-negative cells. The Gram-stain is the basis of bacterial identification. Gram-negative and positive micro-organisms are distinguished using the Gram stain.

Habitat - the place where a microorganism lives. The habitat typically contains all the conditions to either simulate growth or to preserve the organism.

HEPA - High Efficiency Particulate Air - describes the system for filtering (diluting) air into cleanrooms. Standard HEPA filters remove 99.97% of 0.3µm particles.

HVAC - Heating, Ventilation and Air Conditioning - a system for providing air into clean rooms and controlling their classification by removing airborne particles through the use of HEPA filters.

Isolator – Self-contained clean spaces designed to protect product from contamination by room, that exchange air with the surrounding environment only if the air has passed through a filter of at least HEPA quality.

Laminar Airflow - where air travels in either a vertical or horizontal direction at the *same* velocity.

LAF / LAC - Laminar airflow cabinets are designed to direct particles away from the work surface (this is often supported by airflow or smoke studies). The term 'LAF' is becoming increasingly replaced by UDAF or uni-directional air-flow. The terms have different meanings (see **UDAF** and **turbulent flow** below).

Medium (plural, media) - Any liquid or solid material prepared for the growth, maintenance, or storage of microorganisms

Microbial population - Total number of living microorganisms in a given volume or mass.

Microbicide

- The root -cide meaning to kill can be combined with other terms to define an antimicrobial agent aimed at destroying a certain group of microorganisms.
- Bactericide is a chemical that destroys bacteria except for those in the endospore stage.
- Fungicide is a chemical that can kill fungal spores, hyphae, and yeast.
- Virucide is any chemical known to inactivate viruses, especially on living tissue.
- Sporicide is an agent capable of destroying bacterial endospores .

Microflora - Bacteria (including actinomycetes), fungi, algae, and viruses found in a given location. For the human body (and related to this, the majority of the micro-organisms found in the Aseptic Filling Suite), the term **Normal Flora** can be applied. It can also be called resident flora and consists of a variety of microorganisms adapted to the body at the sites of the human body that harbor normal flora which are skin, digestive tract, upper respiratory tract, external genitourinary tract and external surfaces of the eyes and ears. The majority of such micro-organisms isolated are *Staphylococci* and *Micrococci*.

Particle - an object of solid or liquid composition, or both, and of a certain size. It is a small piece of matter with a defined physical boundary. The size and number of particles are critical in order to assess a cleanroom.

Particle counter - a device which measures the number of airborne particles of a given size by passing a sample of air through a focused light source. The presence of a particle causes dispersion of the light and the presence of a particular size can be detected using pre-defined criteria. At BPL two sizes of particles are measures: 0.5µm (a close approximation of the size of a bacterium) and 5.0µm (a close approximation of the size of a human skin cell).

Q10- A relationship for the effect of temperature on a process such that the process rate increases by the same multiple for every 10°C rise in temperature.

Risk assessment – a systematic process of organising information to support a risk decision. It involves the identification of hazards, analysis and evaluation of the risk associated with the exposure of the hazards. This can be quantified to the probability of occurrence of harm and the severity of that harm.

Sanitation - a cleansing technique used to remove microbes or other particles by reducing the level of contamination. It does not produce total kill.

Involves the use of sanitisation agents, which are chemicals/products such as soaps or detergents used as a cleaning technique to remove microorganisms and reduce the level of contaminants.

Soil - Unconsolidated mineral or organic matter on the surface that has been subjected to and influenced by genetic and environmental factors of: parent material, climate (including water and temperature effects), macro organisms and microorganisms, and topography, all acting over a period of time and producing a product - soil - that differs from the material from which it is derived in many physical, chemical, biological, and morphological properties, and characteristics

Spores - Specialized reproductive cell. Asexual spores germinate without uniting with other cells, whereas sexual spores of opposite mating types unite to form a zygote before germination occurs (see also endospores).

Sporicide – A chemical that can destroy or inactivate viruses and all bacteria, fungi and their spores.

Sterile - an absolute term meaning free of all living microorganisms but not necessarily any biologically reactive by-products such as exotoxins or endotoxins.

Sterilisation- Rendering an object or substance free of viable microbes but not of microbial toxins, such as, endotoxin by destroying or removing all viable microorganisms, including viruses. An object cannot be slightly sterile or almost sterile - it is either sterile or not sterile. Control methods that sterilize are generally reserved for inanimate objects

UDAF – unidirectional air-flow. This indicates air moving in streamlines of the same direction but not necessarily at different velocities (for air moving in both the same direction and at the same velocity this is described as **laminar air-flow;** for air moving in different directions this is **non-unidirectional or turbulent air-flow**).

Vegetative cell - Growing or feeding form of a microbial cell, as opposed to a resting form such as a spore. The vegetative cell state is the form in which an organism is able to grow and divide continuously given favourable conditions (although this can also refer to the non-reproductive phase in fungi). Unlike endospores, vegetative cells are relatively poor at surviving environmental stresses such as high temperature and drying

Viable - Alive; able to reproduce.

Water - there are various types of water, categorised in part by their chemical and microbiological states:

- Water for Injection - is the highest grade of water. It can either be sterile or as bulk. There are limits on the number of viable microorganisms and endotoxin levels. It is produced by distillation at BPL.
- Demineralised water - is treated mains water where significant minerals and ions are removed. There are limits for the number of viable microorganisms.
- Mains (or raw or potable water) - is the incoming water to BPL from the water authority. There are limits for the number of, and absence of certain types of, viable microorganisms.

INDEX

Note: major references are set in **bold** and references to illustrations are *italicised*. 't' denotes a table, 'a' an appendix and 'g' the glossary.

CPSIA information can be obtained
at www.ICGtesting.com
Printed in the USA
BVHW030429231020
591515BV00005B/364

9 781781 487686